GIRL'S PASSAGE FATHER'S DUTY

BRIAN & KATHLEEN MOLITOR

Emerald
Books

P.O. BOX 635, LYNNWOOD, WA 98046

D1115163

Emerald Books are distributed through YWAM Publishing. For a full list of titles, visit www.ywampublishing.com or call 1-800-922-2143.

Girl's Passage—Father's Duty
Copyright © 2007 by Brian D. and Kathleen A. Molitor

Published by Emerald Books
P.O. Box 635
Lynnwood, WA 98046

Library of Congress Cataloging-in-Publication Data
Molitor, Brian D., 1952–
  Girl's passage father's duty / by Brian D. and Kathleen A. Molitor.
    p. cm.
  ISBN-13: 978-1-932096-40-8 (pbk.)
  ISBN-10: 1-932096-40-X
 1. Fathers and daughters. 2. Fathers. 3. Parenting. I. Molitor, Kathleen A.
II.Title.
  HQ755.85.M635 2007
  306.874'2—dc22   2007010615

Unless otherwise noted, Scripture quotations in this book are taken from the Holy Bible, New International Version NIV®. Copyright ©1973, 1978, 1984 by International Bible Society. Used by permission of Zondervan Publishing House. All rights reserved. Verses marked KJV are taken from the King James Version of the Bible.

Second printing 2012

Printed in the United States of America

CONTENTS

PART FIVE: CREATING A PLAN FOR YOUR DAUGHTER

PART SIX: NEW HOPE FOR WOUNDED DADS

FOREWORD

THROUGH MORE THAN TWENTY-FIVE YEARS of teaching, counseling, writing, and speaking, I am a firm believer that success starts with a vision and is enhanced by proper planning. In other words, you begin with the goal or desired end in mind and then establish a logical plan to see that vision realized. For example, if you want to go on vacation, you need to first decide upon your destination. How about Hawaii? That makes a nice vision, right?

The vision is only the beginning. From there, the planning process begins and each step in the plan takes you one step closer to your goal. Contact the airlines. Book a flight. Secure a hotel. Purchase new sunglasses. And so on. Before long, your vision becomes a reality.

What I love about *Girl's Passage—Father's Duty* is this: Brian and Kathy Molitor provide us with both a positive vision for our daughters and a complete plan to launch them into successful adulthood. This book wastes no time worrying about what's wrong with children today. Instead, it shows us how to make things right. In it, you learn practical strategies for encouraging your children and even those outside of your home. The concepts of life-long mentoring, intentional blessing, and rites of passage for today's young people are absolutely transformational.

Brian and Kathy write from experience in sharing how having a vision and a specific plan for each child's development has impacted the lives of their four children. In the book, they invite us to share the details of their daughter's own rite of passage and the events leading up to that special night of celebration. Brian shows us fathers that our words, touch, and encouragement serve as catalysts for our daughters' development.

Regardless of your family situation, this book will provide you with a new vision for the young women in your life and a plan to support their transformation into adults. *Girl's Passage—Father's Duty* is part inspirational and part how-to manual, assuring us that it is never too late for a father to make a difference in his daughter's life.

As a father of two daughters, this book had me on an emotional roller coaster with some smiles, some tears, and some great memories. Most of all, *Girl's Passage—Father's Duty* was a reminder of the power of a plan for my daughters' future. You are going to love it!

Dr. John Trent, Ph.D
Stongfamilies.com
Author of *2 Degree Difference* and *The Gift of the Blessing*

THE KING'S DAUGHTER

THERE ONCE WAS A MIGHTY KING who ruled over a vast kingdom. His ever-expanding domain was breathtakingly beautiful: snow-capped mountains, fertile farmlands, pristine streams, and immense oceans brimming with life. Much to the delight of his subjects, the King's world overflowed with countless plants, animals, fish, birds, and other marvelous creatures.

Now the great King loved all of his creation. However, his deepest love was reserved for his children, the young ones who inhabited his lands. Each was precious in his sight. Moreover, each played a unique role in the expansion of the kingdom. Therefore, the King designed a unique plan to insure that each one grew in safety, gaining knowledge and wisdom with each passing day. His brilliant design left little to chance, especially when it came to his daughters. You see, each daughter was assigned a guard who loved and protected her as his own. These gentle warriors served as representatives of the King, sworn to mirror his kindness, goodness, love, and provision.

The process of connecting daughters to their protectors was deeply moving for everyone involved. As each girl took her initial breath, her warrior stood watching. His first act was to lift her aloft in tribute to her King. Next, the warrior held the daughter in his arms, looked deeply into her tiny eyes, and spoke forth his solemn pledge to protect, guide, teach, and love her from that moment on. The plan had never failed before.

One day, it was announced that a new daughter was to be born, and immediately the King called her protector into his presence. Speaking quietly, in solemn tones, the King charged the warrior with his sacred duty. "I have selected you for this vital task," the King announced. "You have all that you need to successfully watch over my daughter. You have been granted many weapons with which to protect her. Your words have power to bring comfort and to ward off fear. Your hands have the power to heal her wounds and to build within her a sense of confidence, so that she can do all that I ask of her.

"And never forget," the King said, "you may also call upon me if you ever become confused about what to do. Ask me for help and I will answer."

The King looked upon the warrior, one of his trusted sons, with pride that only a father can comprehend. Smiling, His Majesty reached forth his mighty hand and touched the warrior gently on his forehead. Wonderful warmth filled the man, imparting wisdom, courage, compassion, and love for the daughter that he had not yet seen.

"Take care of my daughter," His Majesty said. "You have many other duties in this life; however, none is more important than this. Remember, until I send another to take your place, her life is in your hands."

At this, the warrior fell to his knees and softly said, "I will not fail you."

Then the great King said something the warrior did not expect. "For years now, you have been called by many different names. However, in the morning when my new daughter arrives, your name will be forever changed. From then on, you will be called by a most special name. Your new name will be *Father.*"

At this the warrior trembled momentarily, gathered his strength, and then stood ramrod straight.

"Yes, my King," he replied. "This too is a great honor. I am proud to be called Father."

Elated, Father could not sleep much during the night. He could not stop thinking about the changes soon to come into his life. Doubts, fears, and excitement all competed for his mind's attention. This was his first such assignment; however, Father was ready to take on the challenge.

At daybreak, the King's new daughter was born. He named her Purity. By her bedside, in full armor, stood her new Father. Removing his helmet, the willing warrior lifted Purity high into the air, acknowledging the King, and then drew her near his face. For a brief moment, Father saw himself reflected in her eyes and was shaken by the gravity of his calling. Although he realized that she was actually the King's daughter, he instantly loved her as his own.

Suddenly Father's concentration was broken by the arrival of the King's courier bearing an incredible array of unique gifts for the child. Each gift was carefully wrapped and came with specific instructions about when to open it and how, one day, Purity would use it to further build the kingdom. The final gift bestowed was a beautiful ring, a sign that this precious daughter belonged to the King. Soon it was time to take the little one home.

As time passed, Father became Purity's constant companion. Under his loving care the child grew strong, just as her King had planned. The job of watching over her was never easy, as she required constant attention. Not only did Father have to keep track of Purity, but he had to safeguard her gifts as well. Father soon noticed that the more time he spent with Purity, the more his own life's pursuits faded in importance.

The young one learned much from Father's mentoring and example. He also taught her many important things about her unique gifts and how to use them. Father's loving touch and gentle words of encouragement shaped Purity according to the King's plan for her life. Her future seemed secure in every way.

One day, however, a dreadful thing happened. Father had taken the young girl out for a walk near the edge of the kingdom, not far from the place called the Swamp. You see, at the eastern edge of the kingdom lay a small area yet untamed. In this foreboding place, impenetrable briar and tangled trees concealed noxious weeds and oozing mire. Horrible creatures, unlike those found in the kingdom, hid from the watchful eyes of the King's guards.

Father was well aware of the Swamp but was not concerned that any harm would come to young Purity. After all, he and the King's daughter had passed by before without incident. However, on this day, instead of walking swiftly past the distant darkness, Father made a decision that would forever change both of their lives.

"Let's stop for a while," Father said, spreading a blanket for Purity on the lush, green grass. "Just for a moment and then, I promise, we will be on our way."

Purity nodded in agreement, sat down, and opened the large box containing the gifts given to her by the King—she never went anywhere without them. Satisfied that his young charge was safe, the warrior lowered himself into a sitting position, his back against one of the towering trees common to that area. From this vantage point, Father could watch over Purity and could also see the edge of the Swamp. Unfortunately, he could not see the three pairs of eyes peering out of the brush, studying their every move. The eyes, like blazing bullets of fire, belonged to creatures of darkness whose only purpose in life was to steal, destroy, and, if given the chance, kill the children of the King. Father knew from experience that these creatures were never far away. However, he also knew that they were no match for a fully alert warrior. Feeling justified in his decision to rest, Father leaned back against the dark bark of the tree and smiled.

Just a moment's rest, he thought to himself, *and then we will be on our way again.*

Tired muscles wrestled to find peace as his armor, so useful in battle, grew cumbersome. Seeking his own comfort, Father removed his helmet, followed by his breastplate and belt in rapid succession. Propping his shield against the tree and laying his sword on the ground, the warrior slowly relaxed. He then allowed himself the luxury of closing his eyes—just for a moment. Soon, images of pleasant times and faraway places flooded his tired mind. Father's earlier life had been good, and he daydreamed about many things. Trips to distant parts of the kingdom. Battles fought and won. Days gone by and days yet to come. Lost in his own world, Father lost sight of the King's daughter.

Now, this warrior never intended to shirk his duty. Father meant no disrespect to the King, and certainly his love for Purity had never been stronger. However, his head began to nod, and soon he blissfully drifted off to sleep. The young girl, unaware that her protector slumbered, wandered away toward the Swamp—at the worst possible moment. Purity reasoned that if she went too far, Father would warn her and call her back, as he had many times before.

The warm sun, wildflowers, and birdsongs created a dreamlike setting for this young innocent one. She had no idea that in seconds her dream would shatter into a nightmare.

From their place of ambush, the creatures could scarcely believe their good fortune. Not only was the King's daughter meandering toward them, but more important, the warrior that they feared had fallen asleep. Sensing an opening, the foul beasts crept from the shadows and ran toward the girl, picking up speed with each step. When Purity first saw these new creatures, she smiled to welcome them into her world. Goodness was all she had ever known, so she never imagined what was about to happen. Like swift wolves, the beasts smashed into Purity, knocking her down with their initial rush. Instantly the young girl's smile turned to a look of horror. For the first time in her life, the King's daughter felt fear and pain. Too scared to scream, Purity curled up into a ball, covering her face from the terrible scene. She could only hope that her warrior would awaken before she was destroyed.

The creatures circled the girl's motionless body menacingly. They angrily grabbed for her precious gifts that lay scattered on the ground around her. Even these base creatures knew that each gift was a key to the expansion of the King's territory—and the destruction of their own. One by one, they snatched the packages, clawing them to tattered pieces. The first gift ruined was *vision*. If she could not see a great future for herself, then surely she would fall short of the King's plans. Next, they attacked her *virtue* and sense of *self-worth*. Without these, she would spend years wallowing in shame. One creature snarled loudly when he found her gift labeled *hope*. Its cruel brain surmised that without it, she would spend years sickly and weak. Emboldened by the lack of response from her warrior, the demented beasts tore through her gift called *faith* as though it were made of butterfly wings. Then, the largest of the creatures spied the ring upon her finger and howled in sick delight. Realizing that it had been a special present from the King, the monster cruelly ripped the ring from her tiny hand and clumsily pushed it onto the end of its twisted, bloody claw. Then, all three of the creatures cruelly mocked her plight.

"Why doesn't your great King come to save you? He does not love you at all. Your so-called King has left you and forsaken you!" the ugly brutes screamed. "You have wasted his gifts, and you are of no use to him now! You have nothing to live for. Your life is over!" Purity covered her ears but could not block out the destructive voices raging against her.

Tiring of their sick game, the tormentors began their final assault on the child, inflicting nasty gashes on her arms, legs, and face. They stopped occasionally, just to watch her suffer. Moaning softly, Purity's soul silently screamed, *Where is he? Why doesn't Father come?*

Slowly circling, claws extended, the creatures closed in now for the kill. Purity lay battered and bleeding, stripped of her vision, virtue, faith, and hope. Tormented by questions about her King's love and her protector's whereabouts, soon this daughter of the King would be no more.

Just as it is not clear what caused Father to fall asleep, it is also uncertain what caused him to wake up. Perhaps he heard the snarls of the creatures as they pressed their final attack. Perhaps he sensed that Purity was in trouble. Whatever the cause, the sleeping warrior finally awakened. Eyes now opened wide, Father finally grasped the gravity of the scene and leapt into action. The enraged warrior grabbed his sword and ran straight at the enemy. From deep in his chest Father roared out a war cry. This thunderous mixture of righteousness and rage rolled across the field, striking fear into the beasts. As one, the foul creatures turned to face Father, their sworn enemy. A second battle cry from the warrior robbed the brutes of what little courage they had, and at last they turned to flee. The largest of the three grabbed Purity's limp body and ran, dragging her toward the darkness. Hoping to discourage Father, the beast screamed as it retreated, "It is too late. She is too far gone. Why risk your life for her? It is too *late*!"

The carefully chosen words momentarily caused Father to break stride. He wondered, *Could it be too late? Maybe I should just...*

His hesitation lasted less than a second. "Liar!" Father yelled as he pressed his attack. "It is *never* too late!"

Reaching the first creature, Father swung his sword from high to low, cleaving the beast in two. Gaining speed, he overtook the second monster and, without breaking stride, drove his blade deep between its shoulders into its heart. The beast howled, vainly grasping at its mortal wound and breathed its last. Looking up, Father's eyes beheld a terrifying sight. The largest had nearly reached the safety of the thickets, and in his clutches draped the King's lifeless daughter. The enraged warrior knew that unless he was swift, the monster would disappear into the gloom, taking with it all hope of ever regaining Purity.

Glancing back, the ogre realized that Father had awakened too late and would be powerless to stop it. A sneer slashed across its ugly face as the creature gathered itself for its final leap into the protection of the swamp. Sensing victory, the beast rejoiced that it had defiled the daughter of the King and would live to tell the tale. On this day, wickedness had triumphed, and the kingdom would suffer loss. This battle was over...or so it seemed. You see, evil often underestimates the strength, speed, and courage of the King's warriors once they have awakened.

Just as the beast made its final laughing leap, it saw a flash from the corner of its eye. Confused, it turned its head in midair and came face to face with the enraged man. Eyes wide with fear, the beast thrust Purity's body aside and tried vainly to avoid the sword stroke already rocketing toward it.

Twisting in midair, Father's powerful arm swung his sword in a hissing arc. It was the last sound that the creature ever heard. Blade and flesh collided, severing the monster's ugly head from its body. Father's momentum carried him into the cruel briar and rocks of the swamp's edge, tearing his flesh. He too had been wounded in the battle. Shaking himself, the warrior slowly stood and looked down at the slain creature. This demon would never harm another of the King's daughters. Father then wrested the King's ring from the monster's stiffening claws and limped back toward Purity, expecting the worst.

Ignoring his own pain, Father found her lying facedown, motionless on the ground. He was horrified at how badly she had been wounded. "I am too late!" he cried as bitter tears fell onto her blood-soaked garments. "Why did I fall asleep?"

His heart ached at the realization that the beast had been right... Father had awakened too late to save the King's daughter. Falling beside her, the wounded warrior cried out to his King.

"O sovereign Lord, forgive me!" he stammered as a mixture of blood and tears streamed down his face. "I took my eyes off of your daughter, and now she is gone. I am not worthy to be called Father any longer."

Suddenly he heard a sound that momentarily stopped his crying. A faint cry escaped Purity's lips. Miraculously, she was still alive! There was hope! Reaching for her, Father held his breath and waited. Her eyes, tightly closed, finally opened and looked into his.

"Father...where were you?"

The warrior had no answer to give. He could only hold her close and repeat, "I am so sorry. Please forgive me. You are safe now. I will never leave you alone again." Hearing Father's words, Purity's soul calmed, and she began to quietly weep.

Carefully, this wounded warrior drew the battered child close to his chest and held her until her tears subsided. He then gently cleansed her wounds and placed the King's ring once again upon her fragile finger. With darkness approaching, Father picked up this broken daughter of the King and began the long journey home, one step at a time.

PART 1

DADS AND
DAUGHTERS

TODAY'S CHALLENGE, TOMORROW'S CHANGE

THE SIMPLE STORY ABOUT THE KING'S DAUGHTER is just that—a story. Just a tale about a make-believe father who fell asleep on the job. It's not real, or is it? Sadly, the story is as real as can be, and too many children today suffer the effects of a fatherless existence. I wonder what the warrior in the story will say when he once again stands before the King.

"Sorry, King. I was too tired to take care of your daughter..."

"Sorry, King. I was distracted..."

"Hey, I *told* her not to go too far..."

The fact is, when our daughters are born, we fathers are commissioned by God to watch over them, love them, and protect them. No excuses. No exceptions. No sleeping on the job. Now, before any guilt sets in, let us be clear that we all fall short when it comes to raising our daughters. We all drift off. Some of us snooze for only a matter of moments and wake to find our daughters relatively whole. However, for others, slumber becomes a way of life, leaving innocent daughters to face the beasts of this world all alone.

THE PRESSURE ON YOUNG LIVES

As fathers, we must understand that our daughters are susceptible to extreme emotional pressures during their crucial, formative years. Too often, this pressure results in depression, anxiety, fears, obsessive/compulsive behaviors, perfectionism, promiscuity, and a desire to please others, often at the expense of themselves. Here are some alarming statistics: According to the White House Office of National Drug Control Policy, teenage girls not only caught up to their male counterparts in illegal drug use and alcohol consumption but also surpassed boys in smoking and prescription drug abuse. The size of the problem? According to the government survey, in 2004, the last year for which data are available, 1.5 million girls began drinking, 730,000 started smoking cigarettes, and 675,000 began using marijuana for the first time.

The White House Office also points out that adolescent girls who smoke, drink, or take drugs are at higher risk for depression, addiction, and stunted growth. In addition, because substance abuse often goes hand in hand with risky sexual behavior, they are more likely to contract a sexually transmitted disease or to become pregnant.

Advertisers, sensing the vulnerability in young women, target them in campaigns selling sweet-tasting alcoholic drinks, cigarettes, diet pills, and a host of other substances. Television programs push a lifestyle that is anything but wholesome and healthy for our young women. MTV-type programs portray "spring break" experiences as the ultimate good time. Young, impressionable viewers are treated to fast-paced images and pounding music as a backdrop for a host of hip young people happily engaged in binge drinking, dirty dancing, self-exposure, and sexual encounters with near strangers. Predictably, no shots document the morning after or the damage done to precious young bodies, souls, or spirits. Today, our young women are under tremendous, unrelenting pressure to take the wrong path. As in fairy tales of old, unseen creatures, in many forms, threaten these young damsels in distress. The need to be rescued is great; the time is now.

The job before us is not for the faint of heart nor for those whose commitment is weak. Like the creatures from the Swamp, the enemies lie in wait for our daughters, watching for an opening or a sign of weakness. However, they also watch our actions as well. Are we alert? Are we teaching our daughters the truth? Are we there when they need words of love and affirmation? Are we the ones who touch our daughters appropriately, so that they do not seek inappropriate affection elsewhere? As I have already said, none of us will ever get it right all of the time. However, we must now awaken and realize that the farther we allow our daughters to wander, especially during the first two decades of their lives, the greater the chances that they will be victimized.

A daughter who receives her dad's love, time, and attention generally fares well in this life. Conversely, daughters deprived of their father's love, time, and attention are left vulnerable to a wide variety of attacks. This exposure obviously exists in homes where the dad is absent; however, it is also present in houses where a father lives under the same roof yet fails to provide mentoring, words of blessing, healing touch, and prayers for his children.

We must acknowledge that our daughters' lives are not fairy tales with prewritten, happy endings. The threat against each of them is real, and the ending of the story is yet to be decided. In fact, the challenge is so great it will take a hero to save the day. A hero called...Father.

WHY FATHERS SLEEP

As fathers, we have many reasons for our slumber. One of the most common is also the most sinister. We simply get too busy and lose sight of what is truly important in life. This happens when a dad's work or play crowds out his duties at home. He leaves the house early and pours his heart into work. Then, after long hours of toil, he drags himself home, exhausted, drained, needing his "space." For many fathers the visions of corporate success rob their energies and keep them from fulfilling their sacred responsibilities to the children under their care. It is important to point out that this trap of busyness is just as common, and disastrous, for those in "full-time" ministry. What does it profit a man to evangelize the world and lose his children?

In today's world, the rate of divorce continues to skyrocket, which is another cause of fathers missing the crucial years of a daughter's development. Right now, countless children live absent from their biological fathers. This creates an entirely new set of barriers to father/daughter interaction, often making it difficult for Dad to be there when needed.

Of course, we must accept responsibility to provide for our family; however, food, clothing, and shelter will never take the place of a father's time, attention, and regular interaction with his children. Remember, Dad, regardless of the reason or excuse, the end result of a father's slumber is always the same: the King's daughters are left unguarded—and the enemies are lying in wait.

A PERSONAL CONFESSION

I confess that I was one of those dads who, in the early years, spent a great deal of time focused on everything but the development of my own children. Business, ministry, hunting, fishing, and, and, and... took up more of my time, money, and thoughts than I like to admit. However, as my oldest son approached his teen years, a wonderful thing happened: I woke up.

Realizing the need for some deliberate changes, Kathy and I began to prayerfully consider ways we could strategically raise our children by design rather than by default. Naturally, part of our search took us to the Scriptures to see what the original Father had to say. While the Bible is full of admonitions about raising children, one passage truly changed our lives—Malachi 4:6. The message of Malachi is simple: fathers must turn their hearts, minds, and attentions toward their children. The word *turn* in this passage has a variety of powerful meanings: to turn back, to go back home again, to rescue, and to carry again. This beautiful admonition provided the spiritual foundation for our strategy and launched us on a journey to find practical ways of leading our children into successful adulthood.

After months of studying the Bible along with modern-day parenting books, and of exploring how other cultures help their children make the transition into adulthood, we decided upon our own three-part plan. This plan, consisting of lifelong mentoring, intentional blessing, and a rite of passage, became the foundation for my first book on the subject, entitled *Boy's Passage—Man's Journey.* Since that time, the plan has helped each of our children grow into a level of maturity that would have otherwise been impossible.

The plan, in its entirety, is presented here in this book to help you with your own children. Please know that this plan is not all that difficult to implement. Once developed, it becomes a wonderful way of life, requiring just a bit of time and attention to that which truly matters. As a father, I am so glad that I woke up when I did.

WHERE DO WE GO FROM HERE?

For many of us who have daughters, the issue is not "why did we fall asleep?" but rather "what do we do now that we are awake?" This is a father's question. It is the only question worth asking. We must realize that it is never too early for a father (or future father) to create a plan to reach, raise, disciple, and love his daughter. How wonderful to accept our role as mentor, protector, and guide even before a daughter draws her first breath. However, it is never too late for a dad with an older daughter to reconnect, reclaim, and reestablish relationship with her! The past is behind us, and once we realize our mistakes, there is no need to spend any more time dwelling there. It is now time to move on. Here is how Kathy and I did it.

We started by simply dedicating (or rededicating) ourselves to our daughter's well-being. Then we created a plan to bless her life, even if it meant that our own lives would be inconvenienced. Next, we made the choice to accept, comfort, and love her unconditionally, regardless of her age or current situation. As her father, I made the choice to listen to my daughter's dreams and to affirm her plans, thereby providing her with courage and confidence.

As part of our plan, we recognized that when (not if) we failed our daughter in some way, we would always simply ask for forgiveness and keep moving forward, propelling her toward the King's destiny for her life. As her dad, I made a commitment to use my affirming words, appropriate touch, and unconditional love to heal any wounds that she has suffered. Finally, my wife and I realized the need and responsibility to take our daughter before the King in prayer, acknowledging that we were only stewards of *his* precious children.

This plan may sound difficult or complex. It is neither. It is an honor and a blessing to serve God by caring for his daughters in this way. Remember, as fathers, mothers, and mentors, we are powerless to help our daughters only if we fail to try.

A FATHER'S PRAYER

So, Dad, as you read this book, I want you to be encouraged and empowered with a plan to watch over the King's daughters under your care. I assure you that you have the time, talent, and strength to be the warriors that God has called you to be. Let's get started on this journey by having a quick meeting with the King and asking for strength for the task ahead. Let's pray this one together...

Heavenly Father, I want to be the warrior that you have created me to be. At times I have not properly carried out my duties to love, guide, and protect your daughter. At times I have fallen asleep. Please forgive me and take away my shame and sorrow. I bring the precious daughter that you have given me before you, asking that you heal her hurts and restore all that has been lost, stolen, or given away. Help me as I help her to keep moving forward toward your perfect plan for her life. Amen.

Now, men of God, it is time for us to wipe the sleep from our eyes, pick up our swords, and once again walk in the high calling of fatherhood. The past is behind us, and in the days still left there is much work to be done. It is our duty. A father's duty.

We may need a new mindset to accomplish this, so let's now take a look at a father's view of his daughter.

2

NEW LIFE,
NEW DUTIES

WELL, DAD, AFTER MONTHS OF WAITING, your daughter finally arrives. The ride home from the hospital is a mixture of joy and anxiety. You watch the traffic lights a little more carefully today. Precious cargo on board. Soon, you pull into your driveway and gingerly carry your new addition into the house. Exhausted, mother and daughter join together as the baby drinks life-giving milk. You stand by, watching in amazement. Tired. Awestruck. Happy.

Slowly you begin to realize that from this day forward, life will never be the same. You struggle to believe that in a flash this tiny, helpless bundle will speak her first words and take her first, uncertain steps. This eye-opening blast leads you to realize that all too soon her once unsteady feet will carry her out of your world and into her destiny.

You retire to the sanctuary of your favorite chair. Feet up, your imagination now moves quickly through the endless possibilities for your new daughter's life. *What lies ahead for her? Fame? Fortune? Marriage? Heartache? How about grandchildren? Will she be ready?*

Next come some other questions. Tougher ones. The ones that are all about you. *As her father, what role am I supposed to play in her development? Does it really matter what I say and do? Am I ready?*

Your weary mind calls a halt to the endless stream of questions. You head off to bed, hoping that the answers will be there when you wake up. Mercifully, your eyes close and you drift off to sleep.

Soon—too soon—morning comes. At the sound of the alarm clock, you slowly swing your legs off the bed, wipe the sleep from your eyes, and shuffle to the bathroom for your morning shave and shower. Dressing quickly, you walk toward the sound of your wife's voice as she softly talks to your precious daughter. You are amazed at how much your girl has changed.

"Good morning, Daddy! You gonna miss me, Dad? Hey, college is only four hours from here. Daddy, is that a tear in your eye? Thanks for gassing up my car, Dad. Well, gotta go. Orientation is tomorrow morning, and I need to get moved into the dorm tonight. Love you, Mom! Love you, Dad! Bye!"

The door slams loudly as your daughter dashes off into her future, leaving you in the deafening silence. You stand, feet glued to the floor, replaying those questions that ran through your mind twenty years ago. *What lies ahead for her? Fame? Fortune? Marriage? Heartache? How about grandchildren? Is she ready?*

OF COURSE, OUR DAUGHTERS ARE WITH US for more than just one night. However, as a dad with children who have left the nest, I can assure you that is how it seems. We are given a small amount of time to invest in our children before we release them into the world. It is imperative that we make each moment count. I am convinced that a father's influence on his daughter, up to and including the teen years, is immeasurable. This is true whether his influence is positive or negative. The reality is that dads have about eighteen years to lay a foundation upon which our children will build for more than half a century.

3

A FATHER'S JOY

I RECALL THE BIRTH OF OUR THIRD CHILD, Jenifer, with great fondness. The events that led up to her arrival prepared my heart to receive her as the gift from God that she was, is, and always will be. The pregnancy with our second child, Steven, was a true challenge for us all. Kathy spent nearly six months (no, that is not a misprint) in bed due to premature labor and other complications. She finally carried Steven to term, and his birth completed one of the most difficult times of our young married life. Following the delivery, Kathy's doctor strongly suggested that, given the storm we had just weathered, we should not try to have any more children. After much prayer, we felt that God had more children in mind for us, so we left the matter in his capable hands.

Fifteen months later, we believed that Kathy was once again pregnant. Our reactions to the news came from completely different ends of the spectrum. The memories of my wife's six-month confinement flooded her mind, and she wept at the thought of having to endure it again. My response was one of utter joy. I was ecstatic at the thought of having another child, especially a daughter, to join Steven and his older brother, Christopher. When Kathy was not watching, I quietly rejoiced. A short time after that, we swapped emotions when we learned that it was a false alarm; Kathy was not pregnant. For the moment she was relieved, and God used that time to bring healing to her wounded heart. For me, it was torture to think that my hoped-for daughter (I had a hunch...) would not arrive. More than once I cried for the beautiful young girl that God, in his wisdom, had chosen to withhold for just a little while longer before bringing her into our lives.

Later that year we discovered that Kathy was, in fact, going to have a baby. This time, amazingly, miraculously, Kathy's pregnancy was perfect. No premature labor, no mad dashes to the hospital in the middle of the night. Just perfect. Throughout the months leading up to the birth, my lovely wife glowed as women do when they carry within them God's gift of life. After each doctor's visit, we were *assured* of two things. First, that everything was fine. Second, we were definitely having a *boy*. The baby's heart rate, position in the womb, a "pretty sure" ultrasound picture, all convinced the doctors and nurses that a Johnny, not a Jeni, was about to come into this world. My heart said otherwise, but who was I to argue with the doctors?

Now, let me fast forward to the final few minutes of the birth process. This is how I remember it...

I am standing at my wife's side, trying to act calm in the midst of controlled chaos. Nurses dressed in clean, patterned uniforms scurry from one room to the next, checking the progress of numerous mothers-to-be. Our doctor enters the room and, after a quick check, reports that our child will soon be here. From that point on, life in the delivery room takes on an Alice-in-Wonderland feel as fetal heart monitors beep, contractions increase in frequency and intensity, and I try to keep it together. Soon, it all seems wonderfully out of control as the process that our heavenly Father chose to bring his new children into the world plays out. Suddenly, after one final push, the child leaves its sanctuary of the past months and enters a new world of lights, sounds, and deliberate touch. My wife's face, angelic and exhausted, beams. Somewhere, somehow in that moment, I hear a voice—my voice—exclaiming three special words: "It's a GIRL!" Then Jeni takes her first breath and cries a soft cry. The louder cry that fills the room is coming from her father who has never been happier.

My joyful reaction to Jeni's birth would not be typical in every society or for every father today. I think I may know why.

SOCIETY SAYS...?

Light from the television screen flickers off the faces of a family enjoying an evening movie. The film tells a simple story of a young couple coping with all the changes during their first few years of marriage. At one point, the wife tells her husband that a blessed event is going occur—she is pregnant. Chameleon-like, his expressions quickly change from bliss to terror and then back to bliss again. A baby is on the way, and there is much to be done. Subsequent scenes show the couple remodeling, shopping for the crib, diapers, and stuffed animals. After a commercial break or two, the big day arrives. Now the program chronicles the young duo's desperate dash to the hospital where they are met by knowing nurses and the family doctor. Next, swirling scenes show the excitement, anguish, and tension that accompany a baby's arrival into the world. In the final few frames, we hear the soft cry of a newborn, see the tired but happy look on the mother's face, and hear the father proudly proclaim, "It's a BOY!"

Seconds later, we cut to the outside of the hospital where the grinning dad is handing out cigars to several buddies who have gathered to hear the good news. Hands are shaken, backs are slapped, and a jubilant celebration erupts. Above the din, those three words —"It's a boy!"— resound numerous times. The movie fades to black, leaving viewers with a warm and wonderful feeling that all is well. But is it?

Those three simple words send an unmistakable message, not only to the father and his friends but also to the millions of viewers, male and female, watching at home. The message? It is a wonderful thing to have a son born to you and, by implication, a daughter is not quite as great. In other words, boys are better than girls. It is not difficult to imagine the impact of this on the viewers. Fathers and sons pick up the subtle signal that they are special and are worth celebrating. Mothers and daughters, perhaps without even realizing it, absorb the toxic message that they are not quite as special as their male counterparts. Messages such as these die lingering deaths, if they die at all. Sadly, they often take root in the hearts and minds of the hearers, male and female, and slowly grow over time into paradigms, patterns, and lifestyles that are far from what our Creator intends.

As I look back over the past half century, I recall many TV shows, movies, and even cartoons that subtly and, in all likelihood, innocently perpetuated this message. Boys are somehow better than girls. I remember an acquaintance of mine from years ago who shocked me with his comments about his newborn child. When I asked him about the birth, he screwed up his face with the look of a man who was about to be ill and said, "Darn it, I got a *girl.*" He then shook his head in disgust and changed the subject. I was horrified at his lack of appreciation of the gift that God had just given him. He too had bought the lie that somehow boys are better than girls.

This sad perspective is evident in many cultures. However, its tenacious presence is difficult to comprehend, especially among Western societies based upon biblical foundations. I believe that a thorough study of the Scriptures reveals two fundamental truths that, when understood, eliminate a great deal of confusion. First, the Bible does *not* say that gender is irrelevant when considering roles and responsibilities within the church. Neither does it leave the door open for revisionists who want to eliminate any gender references concerning God himself. Second, however, the entire canon of Scripture makes it quite clear that in terms of *value*, women and men are equal. Consider Galatians 3:26–29:

> For ye are all the children of God by faith in Christ Jesus. For as many of you as have been baptized into Christ have put on Christ. There is neither Jew nor Greek, there is neither bond nor free, there is neither male nor female: for ye are all one in Christ Jesus. And if ye be Christ's, then are ye Abraham's seed, and heirs according to the promise. (KJV)

This clearly states that God's love, attention, plans, and fundamental promises are for all people, regardless of gender, by virtue of their humanity. If it is good enough for God, it should be good enough for the rest of us!

WHAT'S YOUR STORY?

If you are fortunate enough to have a daughter born to you, I encourage you to stop for a moment and reflect on your attitude toward her. Is it overwhelmingly positive or is there some disappointment? How did your perspective develop? How has it changed? If you were one of the many men who bought into the lie that somehow boys are better, stop now and reconsider. Then thank God for the high honor of assigning you a daughter to love and protect.

My wife and I love each of our children, boys and girl. Each is special and precious. However, to me, no sweeter words have ever been spoken than "It's a GIRL!" I felt that way on the day of my daughter's birth, and my appreciation of Jenifer has grown exponentially since then. In this next chapter, I want to share some special times that God has used to draw me close to my daughter.

A FATHER'S REFLECTIONS

AT THE TIME OF THIS WRITING, I have been Jeni's father for over eighteen years. During that time, I have been amazed at the way in which God has knitted our hearts together. When life allows me to quietly reflect, a host of powerful images and memories come to mind.

COMING HOME

Since the day my daughter came into this world, I have constantly marveled at her unique qualities. I learned very early that she was definitely different from the boys at our house. As an international business consultant and conference speaker, I have spent much of my life enduring the stresses of travel. Late nights, delayed flights, and loneliness all take their toll, adding much credence to the famous line from *The Wizard of Oz:* "There's no place like home."

Fortunately, these challenges also make coming home a most rewarding event, especially when there are young children waiting. Over the years, I noticed a fascinating routine that occurred whenever I returned from a trip. I would open the door and take just a few steps inside, bracing myself to withstand the onslaught that was soon to come. The first to arrive was usually Teddy, the family dog who barked wildly, announcing to the rest of the house that Dad was home. Next, the boys, who were louder and just a bit wilder than the dog. Somewhere in the background was my dear wife, who had learned to stand aside lest she be trampled by the small army headed my way. My gang of greeters would mob the door and all begin speaking at the same time. Using that sixth sense that only a parent possesses, I could usually decode the simultaneous babble into several distinct messages. Typically, one of my sons would ask, "What did you bring me?"

Another son would latch onto my hand, sleeve, or pant leg and excitedly invite me to come and see his latest invention, creation, or discovery. These often included a new skateboard trick or some sort of small creature that had been captured in the backyard. (Mom was not too wild about these.)

Then the final boy's voice would chime in and get right to the point, "Come on, Dad, let's go play."

However, from somewhere in the crush of this wonderful scene would come a different voice. Gentle. Calm. Loving. It was little Jeni's voice asking an amazing question: "Daddy, how was your trip?"

Those words always thrilled me and convinced me of the astonishing truth that God created our little girls to be different from the boys. Not better. Not worse. But surely different. Despite the fact that Jeni missed her dad as much as the others did, something marvelous inside overrode her own wants and reached into the heart of her tired daddy. More often than not, I shed happy tears when I felt her pure love and concern. After several bear hugs for the boys, I would push my way to Jeni to scoop her up in my arms for a long embrace. Finally, her mom and I would have our moments of reconnecting, and life was good again.

A DAUGHTER'S TRUST

Kathy and I moved our family to the country when the children were still quite young. Our property had a couple of ponds on it, so we often took our young ones swimming in the summer. Usually our times in the water were uneventful. However, I recall one hot day in particular when all that changed. My gang wanted to go for a swim, so after rounding up the usual array of towels, sunblock, flip-flops, and goggles, we headed out to the water's edge. Now, the two older boys, Chris and Steve, had become very good swimmers and could generally fend for themselves. Jeni, at age four, was just starting to get comfortable with the water and usually splashed around in the shallows, never attempting to venture out past her knees. The pond gently sloped away from the shore for a distance of about twenty feet, so there were no sudden drop-offs for this lifeguard dad to worry about. This was important because I was keeping track of two swimmers, one wader, and two-year-old Daniel, who spent much of the time sleeping on the shore next to me.

On that particular day, everything seemed perfect. The Michigan summer sky was bright blue with white cumulus clouds providing occasional shade to protect young skin. Kathy was inside the house resting, and I was on "kid duty." Chris and Steve were having a contest to see who could swim the fastest, Daniel was snoozing in my arms, and Jeni was enjoying her usual wade in the shallows. Life was good, at least for the moment. However, when children are involved, things can change rapidly. In the next few seconds, my joy turned to gut-wrenching fear as events quickly got out of hand.

Seated no more than twenty feet away from her, I suddenly noticed that Jeni had overcome her fear of deeper water and had begun to walk out toward her brothers. Her young mind reasoned that since she could see them standing in water just past their waists, there was no reason that she could not join them. What she failed to realize was that they were much taller than she was, and in just a few more steps she would be over her head, unable to breathe. I immediately yelled for her to stop and, still holding Daniel, ran quickly out to grab my daughter. When she heard my voice, Jeni turned around to face the shore. As she turned, she lost her balance and began slowly backpedaling toward the deep. Quicker than I can tell it, I watched the water climb higher and higher on her little body—up her shoulders, then her neck, until it finally reached above her mouth. One more step backwards and her nose would be completely submerged.

As I entered the water, I noticed two amazing things. First, despite the fact that Jeni knew she was in danger, she never panicked. In fact, her countenance never changed. She maintained a cool, calm look that I have seen on her face many times when the pressure was on. Second, as soon as she turned toward me, Jeni's eyes locked onto mine and never left. Not once did she look at the rising water. Not once did she yell or cry.

Her gaze spoke volumes. She knew that her daddy was there and some-how her special warrior would make everything all right.

In seconds I reached her side, and while still holding her young brother in one arm, I hoisted Jenifer out of the water. Daniel cried because I splashed him. I cried because I was scared half to death. Jeni just smiled and went back to play.

AN ICY DEATH TRAP

It was January, the fifteenth I think. Michigan's long winter had reached its halfway point, so ice and snow were the order of the day. Growing up here, I was used to the cold temperatures that rarely get above freez-ing during that time of year. That particular day was not unusual in any way—except that it was nearly my last one on earth.

I said good-bye to Kathy and took a minute to scratch behind the ears of the newest member of the house, a female English springer named Maggie. This beautiful young pup belonged to Jeni, but her antics had captured all of our hearts. My daughter's joy at her new buddy's arrival was a wonderful thing to behold and made the extra commotion and occasional carpet cleanups well worth it.

I drove down our long gravel driveway, headed to work with thoughts of knocking out several chapters of a book I was writing. The dense woods surrounding our home was quiet with snow, and a hint of sunshine tried desperately to push past the clouds. As I rounded the front pond, I noticed that the aerator I had placed in the deepest part was working overtime to do its job. Its constant stream of bubbles pre-vented ice from forming over a large area in the center of the pond. I had installed the aerator because some years earlier I had lost a lot of trout in that pond to winter kill, a condition that occurs when the snow and thick ice deplete the water of oxygen, thereby killing the fish. Following the short drive, I arrived at my office and went to work on the book.

Typically, I would spend the entire day at work and then make my way back home sometime after five. However, at about one o'clock that day, I felt a gentle nudge inside to go home for lunch. As my truck came around the final bend toward our house, the front pond once again came into view. Driving past, I glanced to my right and looked out onto its frozen white surface. The bubbles gently stirred the water above the deepest part of the pond. Just as I turned my head, a small splash near the edge of the open water caught my eye.

I slowed my truck and looked again. I was shocked by what I saw. There, fighting for her life was Jeni's new puppy, Maggie. Somehow the pup had gotten out of the house, made her way to the edge of the water, and fallen in. Throwing the truck into park, I leaped out and headed to the edge of the pond. The ice near shore was over five inches thick, more than enough to hold a grown man. However, it tapered toward the open water, making it impossible to walk close enough to grab Maggie. After several steps, I dropped facedown on the ice, sprawled on my belly, and began to inch forward toward the frantic puppy. Realizing that I had only seconds before she would slip beneath the surface and be lost in the dark water below, I moved as quickly as I could. A combination of adrenaline and my heavy clothes shielded me from the effects of the cold as I slid across the ice. Soon I was close enough to reach out and touch Maggie, and I strained to take hold of her collar. Try as I may, I simply could not grab her as she floundered in the freezing water. Despite the risk, I knew that I had to go just a little farther forward or I would lose her.

What happened next is more a blur than clear recollection. I remember moving my entire body—just one more inch—then CRACK! Without warning, the ice underneath me gave way, and I plunged face first into the icy water. The shock when I completely submerged caused me to reflexively inhale, burning my lungs with water and shocking my system to its core. As quickly as I had gone under, I bobbed to the surface and gasped for air. Maggie continued to splash next to my face. However, her efforts were getting weaker as the thirty-five-degree water sapped the life from her little body.

My first reaction was to get to the edge and try to pull myself up onto the ice, out of the death trap. With a surge of adrenaline I placed my hands on the ice, shoved hard, and actually pushed myself up so that my waist was clear of the water. Now all I had to do was to fall forward, roll out of the water, and grab the puppy, and the ordeal would be over as quickly as it had begun. If only it had been that easy.

As I began to lean forward, I once again heard the sickening sound of the ice as it broke underneath me, causing me once again to submerge completely. I tried this approach once more with the same horrifying effect. I knew that I was in deep trouble. Then, for a brief moment, I simply hung on the edge of the ice, contemplating my fate. Here I was, completely alone in the worst mess of my life. No one would even hear me if I called for help. The water below me was over fifteen feet deep, and I could feel its numbing effects stealing my strength with each passing second. The warm clothes that had previously protected me from the cold air now worked with the freezing water to pull me down toward my death. I could literally feel my life leaving, starting with my toes and slowly moving up my ankles, calves, knees, and thighs. Soon I would be unable to even attempt to pull myself out. Exhausted, I stopped struggling and tried desperately to see a way out. At that moment, I knew that I was finished. The thought came to me that I had another thirty seconds to live, and then the end would come.

A sense of calm pushed the fear from my mind. Then I felt a little smile come across my freezing face as the irony of my situation hit home. After all that I had been through in my life, I was now about to die less than a hundred yards from my home. How sad. Then, for a brief moment, I considered why I had ended up in such a mess. As an outdoorsman, I knew the dangers of thin ice and never took risks when it came to such things. Why had I done it? For a puppy? Hardly. The world is full of puppies. The unspoken answer quickly came into my mind. I had not risked my life for a puppy; I had risked it for my daughter. Knowing how sad Jeni would be if anything happened to Maggie, I made my choice and was content to live with it, even for just a few more seconds.

What happened next remains a mystery to me. However, just before I slipped under the surface for the last time, I simply reached out my hands as far as they would go on the ice and tried to dig my fingers into something, anything, but there was nothing to grab. My struggles had pushed water onto the surface of the ice all around the hole, and it was slick as glass. Hopeless as it seemed, I somehow found it in me to try to escape the watery grave one more time. As in a dream, I remember letting out a yell that came from somewhere deep inside of me. At the same time, I dug my fingers at the icy surface and pulled with all of my strength. Miraculously, I literally launched out of the water and onto the ice. Gasping for breath, I tried to move my legs and discovered that I could not get them to respond. My lungs ached from the cold as I tried to comprehend what had just happened. How did I get out? To this day I do not know the answer to that question. I do know that despite the fact that I was out of the water, the trial was not yet over. As I lay on the ice, the urge to simply close my eyes and sleep nearly overwhelmed me. I was exhausted! Suddenly, the sound of splashing startled me back to the moment. Maggie! The puppy's paws slapped the surface of the water once more, and then she stopped her struggles. I rolled onto my back and flopped my right arm toward Maggie, hoping to grab her before she disappeared. Amazingly, my fingers hooked her collar, and in an instant she lay next to me, motionless on ice.

Slowly, painfully, I pulled myself to my knees and then to my feet. Scooping Maggie in my arms, I began to stumble toward my home and its life-giving warmth. Finally, I arrived at my back door and found that my hands could not even grasp the doorknob to turn it. I banged the door with my elbow until my wife came to let me in. Her bright smile turned to a look of fear when she realized our situation. She immediately took Maggie and wrapped her in blankets, while I stumbled to the bathtub, turned on the water, and literally fell in, clothes and all. Initially, I felt nothing as the warm water hit my frozen skin. Soon, however, a thousand needles seemed to poke into me, and I nearly passed out. After a while the feeling came back into my body, and deep gratitude flowed forth toward heaven. I was thankful to be alive.

Maggie was rushed to the veterinarian, and after several hours she was tearing around our house again as if she owned it. When Jeni came home from school that day and learned what had happened, she gave each of us at least a year's worth of hugs.

When I think back on that incident, I am amazed at two things. First, I marvel that I made it out of that pond alive. Kathy and I have come to believe that an angel must have pulled me out, for my own strength and hope were completely spent. This helps me know that the King is always watching over his warriors, even the careless ones.

Second, I am intrigued by the tremendous amount of love that I, as a father, have for my daughter. In the past I used to wonder where it came from. Now I know. Such a love was placed in my heart by the King.

I do not tell the story of the frozen pond very often. However, when I do, I always get the same question: If I had it to do over, would I risk my life crawling out on that frozen pond? My answer is simple: Yes. I consider it a father's duty. I have no regrets.

THE DANGER OF FAILING TO PLAN

Fortunately, most of a father's duties concerning his daughter are not as dangerous or unpredictable as my dive into freezing water in January. I am happy to say that life around the Molitor home is usually much more stable than that. One stabilizing factor involves a discovery we made. Over time, Kathy and I learned how important it was to raise Jeni and her brothers according to a plan rather than by chance. An old adage with great implications for child rearing today says, "If you don't care where you are going, any road will take you there." In other words, if you do not have a destination in mind, you never know whether you are going in the right—or wrong—direction. In the next section of the book, we will see ways to create a plan that features lifelong mentoring, intentional blessing, and a daughter's transformational rite of passage.

PART 2

THE POWER
OF A PLAN

5

RAISING DAUGHTERS BY DESIGN, NOT DEFAULT

LET'S TAKE A MOMENT AND THINK ABOUT the generations past and the generations to come. Many years ago, each of us had a great-grandmother and great-grandfather who somehow found each other, in all likelihood got married, and produced the next generation. Our grandparents repeated the process and produced the next generation. Our parents carried on the tradition, and we were born. In the course of living our lives, we met our spouses and produced the next generation of children. From this generation come our grandchildren, who someday will produce great-grandchildren, and so on. Here is the point: each succeeding generation should transfer an inheritance not merely of a name and some material possessions but of positive attributes and qualities.

GENERATIONAL CURSE OR BLESSING

We are all familiar with the concept of inheritance, but too often we view it in terms of houses, land, and other possessions. In reality, each generation has the opportunity to leave a legacy that goes far beyond material goods. This legacy includes such things as strong character, spiritual insights, wisdom, confidence, skills, friendships, and so much more. However, without an intentional plan to do so, it is easy to leave the next generation with more bad than good. Our world is full of people who carry a terrible view of the generation before them. Often, the legacy received is one of anger, jealousy, divorce, abuse, abandonment, addictions, and more. There is even a modern label for this condition.

In some Christian circles, the term generational curse is used to describe this situation where succeeding generations display the same problem, weakness, or tendency as the former. While I believe that there are always some spiritual roots involved and therefore some spiritual activities (such as prayer) that will make a positive difference, I believe that additional factors contribute to the problem.

As parents, we pass on the bad and withhold the good for two fundamental reasons. First, because our hearts are far from the children. This means that we simply spend so much of our lives focused upon ourselves that we miss the opportunity to influence our children in positive ways. The second reason is that we have never taken time to put a plan in place to insure that we are passing on the best that we have to offer to our children. There is truly power in a plan, and that power can be felt for generations. Properly implemented, a plan of this sort helps to insure that future generations will receive a transfer of blessings and not curses.

THE POWER OF A PLAN

Very few things work out the way we would like them to unless we have a plan in place to manage them. Even then, plenty of variables exist, but a plan is a great place to start. Imagine, for example, what would happen if a family tried to go on a week's vacation without any planning. What if everyone just jumped in the car and started driving? Chances are that at the end of the first day the family would have no place to stay and probably nothing much to do. Even if by a great stroke of sheer luck the family ended up at a nice place, a resort perhaps, they would be ill-equipped to enjoy it. The sunscreen, golf clubs, proper clothes, swimsuits, money, etc., would have all been left behind in the lack of planning. In like manner, when we fail to plan strategically for our children's growth and development, we put at risk something infinitely more valuable than a vacation—we jeopardize their future. We can do better than that. We *must* do better than that!

PLANNING FOUNDATIONS

For most people, planning is an extremely common activity. Getting dressed in the morning, taking a trip to the grocery store, and arranging work schedules all involve planning. Not only do we plan, but also we use a host of devices to keep us on track as we go about our day. Palm pilots, day planners, calendars, and even hastily scrawled sticky notes all serve as reminders that we have tasks to perform and goals to accomplish.

Planning, in its most basic form, is extremely simple. Set a goal and then determine what steps are needed to achieve that goal. Using this foundational approach to planning, people have accomplished seemingly impossible tasks. Raging rivers are spanned by complex suspension bridges. Human beings explore and then return from outer space. Diseases are cured by deliberate, painstaking research. And in perhaps the ultimate test of planning, entire families actually get to church on time...occasionally.

Few people would dispute that without a systematic, comprehensive plan, little ever gets accomplished. However, if that is true, we must ask a very basic question: Why don't we use this same deliberate approach in raising our children?

HOW TO GET STARTED

Webster's defines the word *plan* in this way: "to design; to devise a diagram for doing, making or arranging. To have in mind as a project or purpose. An outline; a diagram; a schedule; a map."

As a parent or mentor, you begin the planning process by simply thinking about those qualities that you hope to see in your daughter as she grows. I suggest that you literally write down a list of the attributes of successful young women. Your list will include what you hope to see in your own woman-in-the-making in terms of her growth physically, spiritually, emotionally, and vocationally and in other areas as well. Hygiene, social awareness, grooming, relational skills, manners, financial management, compassion for the less fortunate, and a host of other subjects should also be considered. In addition, you will need to assess what types of support your child will need from you and other trusted adults in order to develop a healthy self-image.

Once all of these concepts are identified, then you have a vision of what you hope to see in your daughter as well as some idea of what it will require from you to bring that about. From there, you create your final plan. The three general foundations for your plan will be lifelong mentoring, intentional blessing, and, ultimately, a rite-of-passage event to help launch your child into adulthood. Here is how this works.

PUTTING THE PLAN INTO ACTION

First and foremost, we must understand that each child is unique, equipped from birth with special gifts, talents, and tendencies. This is vital to grasp, especially if you have more than one child under your care. Here is why. One child may excel in schoolwork, while the next may struggle just to keep up with her peers. One child may be a gifted musician, but the next cannot sing or play an instrument of any kind. One may be a star athlete, and yet, her younger sibling wants nothing to do with sports. As a parent or mentor, you must show your children that although they differ in skills, interests, and abilities, they all have equal value in your eyes. If you favor a child based on her performance or certain field of interest, you will do a great disservice to the other children involved.

As you implement your plan, I strongly suggest that you never try to make one size fit all. Instead, customize the plan for each child based on her special gifts, abilities, and efforts. No daughter needs to hear that she is not quite as good as, as smart as, as diligent as, or as any other thing *as,* her sister, neighbor, or some other young person. Comparisons by parents or mentors are always painful and will be perceived as curses, not blessings, by the very children whom these adults hope to motivate.

THE KEYS TO YOUR PLAN'S SUCCESS:
COMMITMENT, TIME, AND PRAYER

In the purest sense, three keys determine the success of your strategic plan. They include your sincere commitment to the plan, a sufficient amount of time spent with your child to implement the plan, and prayer throughout the process.

For a moment, let us focus on your commitment and the time it will take to make it all happen. The best plan in the world will *not* change any child unless a parent or other mentor takes the time to implement it. I am convinced that the first thirteen to eighteen years of a young person's life are the most crucial in terms of the child's ultimate success in this world. We must be there to guide our children using the simple tools discussed in this book.

Remember, your commitment to your daughter will prove life-changing, regardless of her age. For some parents, this deliberate approach to parenting may initially seem a bit overwhelming. However, I assure you that it is much more desirable to wrestle with the development of a plan now than to try to unravel a mess later due to the absence of a plan.

This is where prayer, the next key, comes in. People of faith understand the wisdom of inviting the Creator of the universe to participate in our lives and in the lives of our children. One simple prayer puts things in motion that otherwise would never have happened. A life of prayer opens doors for our children that otherwise would have remained closed. Remember, while this book addresses the roles of fathers, mothers, and other mentors in the lives of daughters, it does so with the full understanding that children themselves belong to their Creator. We are only stewards, wonderfully assigned with caring for God's daughters and sons during the short time that we have together.

We can and must develop lifestyles that include prayer for and with our children on a daily basis. The practice of saying grace before meals and prayers before bedtime not only brings God's blessing but also provides our children with a model of spiritual awareness for them to follow. In addition, we need to pray for our children whenever they experience any sort of problem, illness, or crisis. I realize that some parents may not be comfortable praying for and with their children; however, this is a very important aspect of a godly plan. More on that later. Remember, even if your plan starts out slow and small, you will still be glad that you started. In the following chapters, we will explore the foundational elements of the plan in detail. Are you ready? Come on, Dad, let's go.

6

LIFELONG
MENTORING

THE FIRST PART OF THE PLAN is called lifelong mentoring. This is an approach to parenting wherein fathers, mothers, and other mentors intentionally teach a host of life lessons to the young ones under their care. This teaching or mentoring process begins very early and continues throughout the life of each child who will, in turn, mentor, teach, and train members of the following generations. Without a deliberate plan for mentoring, parents miss many vital opportunities to teach children life lessons, character qualities, and skills.

THE ORIGINAL MENTOR

Actually, the term *mentor* comes from an ancient Greek tale about Odysseus, who leaves his son Telemachus under the care of a man named Mentor. This surrogate dad faithfully protects and teaches the boy about life in his father's absence. Today's mentors come in many shapes, sizes, ages, genders, and colors. They are called by many different names. First and foremost, they are called *dads* and *moms*. Despite some reports to the contrary, our world is still filled with many parents who are deeply dedicated to the development of their children. Other mentors include youth pastors, coaches, teachers, grandparents, stepparents, aunts, uncles, older brothers and sisters, foster parents, and adoptive parents.

There are two foundational truths about mentoring as part of an overall plan to raise successful daughters. First, mentoring, teaching, and training are all vital elements of every young female's life. Each girl comes into the world ignorant of the dangers around her and oblivious to her own abilities and options. Early experiences with pain and pleasure provide some framework for survival but do little to help the child reach her full potential. It is the quality and quantity of instruction from others, especially her father and mother, that largely determines the girl's eventual maturity and success.

Second, in the absence of positive adult role models, young females will try to find their own role models or mentors. The desire to be under the care of someone stronger and wiser is very powerful. It should be. God put it in us as a means to draw us to our fathers, mothers, and other mentors committed to our development. The absence of positive role models, especially a *father*, creates a void that will be quickly filled by someone less qualified and less desirable.

HOW MENTORING WORKS

Successful mentoring is a blend of close relationships and deliberate lesson plans. Time spent together inevitably puts teacher and student in the most fertile learning laboratory of all—life. If you are fortunate enough to realize the importance of intentional mentoring before your daughter is born, your plan will already be in its early stages on the day that she enters this world. However, for most of us, we wake up to this reality after our daughters have already arrived. In fact, many of us realize the need for a parenting strategy only after we experience the first crisis with our child. Remember, it is never too early or too late. Just start where you are now.

Here is how it works in the most fundamental sense. A mentor sits down and prayerfully makes a list of the life lessons and character qualities that he wants his daughter to experience and/or demonstrate. From that moment on, the mentor (usually dad and mom) will use the list to insure that he is deliberately teaching the child about such things. For example, let's say that on your list are the character qualities of industriousness and perseverance. Your vision then is to see your child grow up with a strong work ethic and to never quit until a goal is accomplished. Now the mentoring begins. As soon as your daughter is able to comprehend, you begin to talk to her about the joy of hard work and the pride of accomplishment. Encourage the child to observe and participate with any home repair or chore that is safe for her, such as washing dishes, caring for pets, or helping dad patch a hole in the wall. Even when they are very young, our children can be involved in grown-up projects. They can bring tools, hold a flashlight, put away the clean pans, and so on. For youngsters, the tasks should not be too difficult, nor should they take too long. As the children grow, both the complexity and duration of projects can increase. Throughout the process, the parent simply talks with the child about what is being done, why it is being done, how it will benefit the family, and why it is important to finish a task once it is begun. Other potential lessons that spring from such tasks include the importance of doing a quality job, how to clean up afterward, and how to take pride in a job well done.

A lesson about perseverance for young children can be further strengthened by reading or telling appropriate stories such as *The Little Engine That Could.* For those of you that missed it during your childhood years, this story tells of a heroic little train that saves the day by hard work and perseverance. Its unfailing confession, "I think I can, I think I can, I think I can...," plants wonderful seeds in the fertile minds of young girls and boys who will someday need to persevere through life's trials. Of course, you are not going to get too far with this bedtime story if your daughter is a teenager, so is the lesson lost? Not at all. You simply adjust your teaching/mentoring approach to another level. For older children, you would forgo the book and simply share with them real life examples of hard work and perseverance. Corrie ten Boom's powerful story of survival will inspire any young person. In fact, the world is full of women and men who demonstrated these wonderful qualities. Michael Jordan failed to make his high school basketball team in his sophomore year and went on to become one of the greatest players of all time. His secret? Hard work and perseverance. The life stories of people like Queen

Esther, Thomas Edison, Abraham Lincoln, Margaret Thatcher, great missionaries and adventurers like Sir Henry Morton Stanley and Dr. David Livingstone, and a host of others will motivate young people with the same simple keys to success—perseverance and hard work.

A PERSONAL EXAMPLE

One of the basic life skills that I wanted my daughter to learn was how to enter a store, interact with clerks, and make her purchases. Basic stuff, but essential to success as an adult. When she was younger, I had Jeni accompany me into stores to simply observe the process of buying goods. On our way back home, I would explain why I smiled and called the clerk by name. In addition, I would provide the rationale I used to choose one brand of product over another. Finally, I told her about the options of check, cash, or credit card that I considered when paying for the product.

Once Jenifer got older, I had her go into the store with me, told her what I wanted to buy, and then had her analyze the products and prices to see which we should choose. The next step was for me to give her enough money to pay for the product so that she could interact with the clerk herself. In the beginning, this was scary stuff for an eight-year-old who could barely see over the counter. However, after a few initial tongue-tied attempts, Jeni developed confidence and learned vital lessons about treating others with respect, the value of money, the importance of comparative shopping, and many other life principles.

Regardless of which life lesson we hope to teach, the process is always the same. Kathy and I simply watch for the appropriate teaching opportunities to arise. We always try to pull the positive lessons out of any situation, even if the situation itself is a negative one. Recently one of Jeni's casual friends broke a commitment to our daughter in order to go to the movies with another classmate. After Jeni's initial anger and hurt subsided, we used the situation to discuss true friendship, the importance of keeping one's word, and the need to guard one's heart to avoid unnecessary pain.

MENTORING MUST CHANGE AS OUR CHILDREN GROW

It is vital for parents, especially dads, to realize that their approach to parenting and mentoring must change as their children grow. During our children's early years, we must provide a great deal of direction and decisions for their lives. Why? Because they simply don't have the maturity to make wise choices on their own at that age. *However,* as our children grow and mature, we *must* change our approach to parenting. This means that instead of telling them what to do, we must teach them what to do. Instead of unilaterally setting rules, we work with them to establish boundaries and guidelines that help them achieve their own goals for life. This means that at times, we even let our daughters and sons make decisions that will cause them to fail. We must watch to see that they don't cause themselves or others harm, of course. However, the reality is that in a matter of eighteen years or so, our children will walk out from under our authority and into their own destinies. Once away from home and our watchful eyes, they will make nearly all of their own decisions. Countless young people who grew up in strict, "good" homes end up making horrible decisions about drugs, drunkenness, sexuality, and more as soon as they escape the confines of home. Why does this happen? Because we controlled every aspect of their lives (perhaps thinking that was in their best interest) right up until the moment that they walked out the door. Suddenly, the child goes from a life of being completely controlled to a life of complete freedom. This invariably leads to a multitude of wrong and sometimes painful choices. How much better it is for us to train our children to make wise decisions while allowing them increasing freedom as they grow and mature. I am convinced that most teenage rebellion is caused by parents' failure to discern when to empower and release their children. The "rebellion" is actually a pushing away from excessive control and insufficient respect for the transition that God is making in a child's life.

THE BOTTOM LINE ON MENTORING

Mentoring moments can happen at any time for the simple reason that life lessons are everywhere. The obvious keys to success for any mentoring relationship are time together, open communication, and strong relationships between a mentor and his or her learner as they focus on predetermined life lessons.

Clearly, the onus is on the father, mother, or other mentor to establish both the relationship and the schedule for ongoing interaction with the children in their lives. By the way, do not worry about the young person's response. It will be overwhelmingly positive. Today's youth are full of questions about life, relationships, love, finance, nature, and a host of other subjects. They just need someone around who is willing to help them explore the answers.

Those of us who have raised young children remember the endless streams of "why" questions that seemed to diminish with age. At one point, I assumed that the rate of questioning slowed or even ceased because the young ones had gotten most of the answers they were looking for. I now wonder whether the questions stopped because, in our own busyness, we quit answering. This needs to change now.

As fathers, we have the opportunity and obligation to teach the foundations of life to the next generation, starting with those in our homes and then radiating out into our churches and communities. If we simply create a plan and set aside time for mentoring, our insights will prepare these young people not only for their transition into adulthood but also for the rest of their lives.

7

INTENTIONAL
BLESSING OF A
FATHER'S WORDS

 THE SECOND PART OF THE PLAN involves the concept of intentional blessing in three forms. These are affirming words, appropriate touch, and prayer. The Bible is filled with examples of how each was used to transform lives. Let's explore some, starting all the way back at the beginning.

IN THE BEGINNING...

The Bible tells us that in the beginning God was confronted with a situation that, to any of us, would have seemed impossible. Genesis 1:2 describes the earth as an empty, formless mass of darkness. Not much to work with, but for an all-powerful God it was all in a day's work. Well, six days' work.

I find it fascinating that with an infinite number of options available, God chose to deal with the chaos in a very simple manner. Instead of releasing the energy of a thousand nuclear warheads to reshape the very molecular structure of the mess that we now call earth, he simply poke the right words, and miracles happened. Believe it or not, we earthly fathers have a similar opportunity to use carefully selected words to bring order into the often chaotic lives of our children.

THE FIRST BLESSING IN HISTORY

The creation of humanity. Just imagine the scene on that amazing day. Surrounded by the beauty of Eden, our heavenly Father has just finished creating the first human. Adam stirs on the warm grass and takes in his initial breath. The rush of life-giving air fills his lungs and sets off an amazing chain of internal processes for the first time in all of eternity. The man's heart begins to pump blood into each tiny capillary of his body. Muscles contract, stretch, and flex. Brain waves and miles of nerve fibers begin to register and catalog each marvelous new sensation. Air, rushing into his nostrils, carries the fragrance of flowers bursting forth from the fertile soil. Then comes another new sensation for Adam that we know as *sound*. Invisible waves emanating from a thousand sources begin to wash over the tiny bones and into the canals of his ears. Wind in the trees, birds singing, a friendly splash of water nearby, all are logged into Adam's mind. Now this new man is ready for the final stage of his awakening. Slowly, eyelids raise and the light gently sends his optic nerves into a frenzy of activity. As they quickly adjust, Adam takes in the indescribable beauty of Eden, the place his Father—our Father— has made for him. The colors are breathtaking. Bright sun, blue sky, and green plants all fill Adam with the wonder of a child.

The marvelous carnival for Adam's senses continues unabated until he hears a new and different sound. This sound is quiet yet irresistible. Adam turns his head to see what all humans, deep within, continue to long for.

A FATHER ON HIS KNEES

The key to what Adam saw is found in Genesis 1, verse 28. Here we discover that the very first act of our God toward humankind was to *bless*. Once we understand what sort of blessing was given, we get a deep appreciation for the love of our heavenly Father. The original Hebrew word that we translate as *blessing* is *barak,* which is a root word meaning "to kneel." It refers to an act of adoration, in which one greatly praises and salutes another. Now, if your view of God is of a cold, vengeful ogre, this will be a very difficult passage for you to reconcile in your mind.

But if you are at least willing to consider another perspective, this image will thrill you.

In reality, God can be most accurately viewed as a heavenly Father who longs for fellowship with his children. How do I know? Because according to the Scriptures, what actually happened on Adam's first day was this: he turned his head and saw his Creator actually *kneeling* beside him. Adam looks full into the face of his heavenly Father. When their eyes meet, there is an instant bond of love between them. No walls. No shame. Just love. Therefore, Adam's first view of his God and Father is summed up in one Hebrew word. *Barak.* Kneeling, loving, and adoring. Of course, God did not bow to worship Adam. Instead, he bent a knee to bless him, as any proud daddy would. Just picture it. Here was God himself, kneeling at the side of his "newborn" child, simply adoring him. Like a modern-day father, face pressed against the hospital's nursery window to get a better look at the marvelous creation that bears his likeness, so God looked at his child and came to a profound conclusion. My new creation is *very* good. The heavenly Father blessed his son with his words, his countenance, and his very posture. What a great model for us to follow.

A FATHER'S BLESSING

Now we can move to the New Testament for more insights about the concept of blessing. In Matthew 19:13, we learn that Jesus blessed the little children. The word *blessed* in that passage is the word *eulogéo,* which means "to speak well of." From this we learn that a New Testament blessing occurs when one speaks words of encouragement and affirmation to another. Never is this concept of blessing more powerful than when a father utters positive words to his daughter, regardless of her age. To think that our words can be used to actually set our children apart for holy purposes is truly awesome and must not be taken lightly. Many wonder if simple words can really be that important. Without question! In the book of Proverbs, King Solomon tells us that our words literally have the power of death and life in them. The disciple James reminds us that both blessing and cursing can come from our mouths. For this reason, it is imperative for fathers, mothers, and other mentors to learn about the power of their words and to use that power to bless the young women in their lives.

KEYS TO BLESSING WITH OUR WORDS

Without question, a blessing is passed on whenever a respected elder speaks words of encouragement and affirmation to another, especially a child. The words used in a true blessing *always* build up the young woman by addressing something *positive.* This involves some aspect of her life including her skills, talents, efforts, abilities, physical appearance, or activities. A blessing is also conveyed when a father and other mentors confirm their unconditional commitment to the young person's welfare.

I want to be very clear that a blessing is not something reserved solely for outstanding performances by the best and the brightest young people. In fact, often those appearing to have the least amount of natural talent need to hear words of blessing the most. True blessing can be spoken over *every* young person once you know what to look for. Far too many fathers are quick to point out faults and slow to identify strengths in the young people around them. These careless words become curses that cripple the very identities of their children.

THREE CONCERNS OF EVERY DAUGHTER

I am thankful that I learned about intentional blessing when my daughter was very young. It became clear that well-chosen words, appropriate touch, and prayer developed both her confidence and her character, so it was easy to continue in this approach to parenting. As time went by, I came to realize that most children struggle with three universal concerns: their appearance, their acceptance by others, and their abilities. As a father, your intentional blessing can overcome each of these concerns. Here is how.

Intentional Blessing about Appearance

If you take a moment to reflect, you will likely recall extended times in front of the bathroom mirror, discovering things that you did not like about your appearance. Remember, each child has heard or thought that they were plagued with at least one thing horribly wrong with his or her body. Words of blessing and affirmation from a respected elder can cancel the perceived curse of imperfection and replace it with a calm sense of self-worth.

Armed with this belief, I spent years encouraging each of my children in these areas, especially Jeni as the only girl in the family. In

Jenifer's case, I started with the issue of appearance for one primary reason—her height. In her early years in school, Jeni was always the tallest child in her class. Not just the tallest girl but the tallest child. In fact, for several years, she stood inches above even the tallest boy in her school. Her growth has leveled off now, and as a young woman, she stands nearly six feet tall. Realizing that her height could become an issue of concern for her, I made a conscious effort to speak a blessing over her physique each time I thought about it. I would tell her what a blessing it was to be tall (like her dad was...) and to be proud of how God had formed her. I am thrilled to report that to this day, she walks gracefully with her head held high.

It breaks my heart to see other tall girls who limp through life, slump-shouldered and eyes lowered as if an apology were needed because of their height. How sad that a father or mother failed to bless them in this important area. What an opportunity for them to do it today.

Acceptance by Others

As our daughters grow, they will naturally become interested in friendships and especially in relationships with members of the opposite sex. This is normal, natural, and—despite the frustrations that accompany it—part of God's plan. (Honest, Dad, it is.) In like manner, boys become interested in girls at just about the same age, which sets up some interesting dynamics. This leads to the first bumbling phone calls, instant messages, and clumsy first dates...for some girls. Others have to wait on the sidelines, which can be a mixed blessing. I happen to believe that much of the dating that takes place in the teen years is a recipe for disaster. Commitments are made and broken overnight, lies are told, tender hearts are shattered, sexual experimentation takes place in the name of "love," and for many the whole process provides much more pain than joy. All too often, young girls are drawn toward the dating scene because they want to be accepted by a male, young or old. Those who fail to feel accepted by their fathers too often look to male peers to fill that need. I am very happy that Jeni's high school years were good ones. She was an excellent student, was a fine athlete, worked at a big corporation as a co-op student, and happily spent the vast majority of her free time at home. Why? Because she knew that she was loved, accepted, and valued by her family, especially by her dad and mom. Over that four-year period, we observed that many of her female friends ran from one bad "relationship" to the next, sacrificing their self-esteem, principles, and bodies on the altar of acceptance. We dads can safeguard our daughters from these traps with our intentional blessing.

Intentional Blessing of a Child's Effort and Ability

Growing up, most of us questioned our ability in a variety of areas. Whether it was playing a sport, public speaking, or some other challenge, we wanted to do well but often fell short of our goals. Failure often resulted in humiliation and rejection by others. Realizing this, I wanted my daughter to have the confidence to participate successfully in any vocation or activity she chose. Therefore, I exposed her to a wide variety of experiences designed to increase her confidence and to encourage her to overcome any natural fears of failure. I taught her to fish, to shoot a gun, to play sports (not just "girl" sports but also football, paintball, and more), and to always try her best. When Jeni participated in any activity, I was careful to encourage her *efforts,* not just her accomplishments. In this way, she learned that her father was thrilled to have her participating and learning and that my approval was not based on her being the best.

In like manner, I always encourage Jenifer to speak her mind. Why? Because so much of this world seems determined to keep women from expressing themselves. This is true in some schools, businesses, and even in some of our churches. I wanted my daughter to know that God would use her to speak truth and to change lives, just as he would her brothers or anyone else.

Over the years, I have watched with great pride as Jenifer has spoken at various events with grace, conviction, and a wonderful anointing often reserved for those much older than she. The most recent example of this occurred at the funeral of her beloved grandfather, Grandpa Hayes. Each member of our family was invited to pay tribute to Kathy's dad during the service. One by one, our children walked to the podium and shared deep feelings about the man who had touched their lives in many ways. The three boys went first, and each made me extremely proud. Next came Jenifer, and I silently hoped that she would not falter under the emotion of the moment. I need not have worried. This fine young woman spoke with the maturity of someone twice her age. She slowly scanned the audience, making eye contact and rarely looking down at her notes. Her well-chosen words brought both smiles and tears to those in attendance as she skillfully unlocked precious memories of her grandpa. When she finished, Jeni walked back to her seat and quietly took her place next to Kathy. Even during such a time of significant loss for our family, I could not help but recognize that God himself was grooming the next generation for his own powerful purposes. As a father, I was glad that my words of encouragement over the years had helped to release the wonderful gifting within her.

CALLING THOSE THINGS THAT ARE NOT AS THOUGH THEY WERE

At times, you need to follow the pattern of God himself who, according to the Bible, calls things that are not [yet] as though they already were (Romans 4:17). In other words, you will need to look past present deficiencies and bless that which lies deep within a child, waiting to be revealed. Here is an example of what I mean. Since she was very young, Jeni loved music, especially singing. Realizing how important this was to her, I purposed to support her all the way. No matter how squeaky her voice, I listened lovingly and applauded wildly at the conclusion of her songs. Over time, her voice grew stronger, and she learned to accompany herself on the piano. If I had not been intentional about my words of blessing, I could easily have discouraged her and caused her to give up any future attempts at singing or music. Fortunately, I spoke blessings only to her efforts, not her results. As her father, I complimented Jeni on anything and everything that she did well, rather than berating her for what she did not do well. The result? Today she is a gifted singer and musician. She even writes songs that bring me to tears with their beautiful words and melodies. My small investment of blessing has reaped a huge dividend in her music.

FOUR THINGS THAT EVERY FATHER MUST LEARN TO SAY TO HIS DAUGHTER

A father's spoken words cost nothing and yet can have such a priceless impact upon a daughter's life. After working with fathers for many years, I conclude that there are four things that every dad *must* learn to say to his daughter. Ready? Here they are:

I love you.
I am proud of you.
I am sorry.
Please forgive me.

Why are these so important? Because we are created by our heavenly Father with a desire to be loved, especially by our fathers and mothers. This is literally built into the human soul and must not be ignored. A father must sincerely tell his daughter on a regular and ongoing basis that he loves her.

Next, we all make mistakes in life. And since raising daughters is part of life, every father will say and do things that hurt them. When, not if, that happens, we must be quick to utter the words, "I am sorry." Did I mention that the words must be sincere? Of course they must. As fathers, we are in positions to bring healing, joy, and peace to our daughters' lives. When we fall short, the least we can do is acknowledge it, apologize, and do our best not to let it happen again.

Finally, an apology is one thing; however, when it is coupled with a request to be forgiven, it becomes a life-changing event. We do not lose respect by asking our daughters to forgive us; we gain it.

Now, Dads, let's practice. Say them with me, filling in your daughters name each time:

(Your daughter's name), I love you.
(Your daughter's name), I am proud of you.
(Your daughter's name), I am sorry.
(Your daughter's name), please forgive me.

Well done, Dad. Now let's explore ways that we can add the blessing of touch to our words.

8

INTENTIONAL BLESSING OF A FATHER'S TOUCH

IT IS TIME TO INTRODUCE INTO OUR PLAN the concept of intentional blessing through appropriate touch. Once intentional blessing becomes a way of life, fathers look for every opportunity to affirm their child through the use of encouraging words, appropriate touch, and prayer. This means that as a parent you spend more time looking to catch your daughter doing something right than looking to catch her doing something wrong. This may be a life-changing adjustment, not only for your daughter but also for you. In this environment, encouragement replaces criticism, blessings replace angry words, and hands are used to administer life-giving touch rather than harm.

GENUINE VS. COUNTERFEIT BLESSINGS

When federal agents are trained to spot counterfeit money, they undergo a fascinating training process. Instead of studying fake bills, the agents spend countless hours studying *real* money. Their education focuses on familiarity with boxes of actual bills in various denominations. The agents-in-training make use of multiple senses during this process. Touch, smell, sight. Over and over again. Pick up a bill, look at it, handle it, crinkle it, and listen to the sound the paper makes when it bends. After what must seem like years, the instructors slip a phony bill into the process and then watch what happens. As with the others, the agents pick up the counterfeit for close examination. It certainly looks legitimate. The writing is all there. Nothing too unusual about how it feels. And yet...something is just not quite right. Eventually, a flaw is detected, and the bill is rejected as a fake. The secret to the agents' success is that they become so familiar with the genuine article that a counterfeit becomes easy to identify.

In much the same way, a father's genuine touch and sincere words of blessing will guard his daughter from the "counterfeits" that she will likely encounter later in life. For this reason, I take every opportunity to apply this knowledge to my interactions with my daughter. Ever since Jeni was born, I used appropriate touch as a means to familiarize her with the genuine, wholesome touch that a woman of any age should expect from a man. When my daughter was little, I held her in my arms. As she grew, I looked for opportunities to hug her, briefly stroke her hair, playfully wrestle, and so on, to have appropriate physical contact with her. In addition, Jeni rarely walked by me without hearing me say words of encouragement, affirmation, and blessing. I often mentioned her beauty and talents and confirmed God's plan for her life. Finally, I was never stingy with the words "I love you."

What is the point of it all? Simple. Just like federal agents learning to identify counterfeit money, Jeni needed to learn how to spot the fakes that could someday come into her life. I remain convinced that because my daughter has felt the loving touch of her father and heard him sincerely say "I love you" countless times, she will be able to spot a fraud. In other words, when some young man comes into her life with bad intentions, she will instantly go on high alert. Should he touch her inappropriately, it will simply feel wrong. Moreover, should the wrong young man call to her with the same words that I have used so many times to bless her, it won't have the same effect. "I love you" coming from a young man with bad intentions will sound like fingernails scratching on a blackboard to my daughter's trained senses. This is more than an option for a dad. It is a father's duty.

THE POWER OF TOUCH

I truly marvel at God's wisdom and creativity when he made our hands. We use them countless times each day with scarcely a thought about their dexterity, flexibility, and sensitivity. Each hand contains twenty-seven bones and twelve muscles. They await our unspoken commands to lift, carry, twist, tap, pound, shake, type, hold, and execute a thousand other tasks. Obviously, these silent servants make life much easier for us. However, God intended for us to use our hands not only to meet our own needs but also to meet the needs of others, to bestow upon them the blessing of touch.

Scientific research continues to show amazing connections between touch and development in both animals and humans. Years ago, psychologist Harry Harlow, experimenting with infant monkeys, proved that lack of physical touch caused immense problems for the young primates. Amazingly, severe emotional and behavioral problems occurred in young monkeys that could see, hear, and smell their parents *but were unable to touch them*. Those deprived of touch became extremely retarded in their behavior and fell into patterns of constant grooming, self-clasping, social withdrawal, and rocking.

Of course, we are not monkeys, so does this research have any bearing on the human race? Without question. One of the most striking examples of this was discovered in Romania, where long-time communist dictator Nicolae Ceausescu's ruined policies resulted in countless orphans kept in near isolation for long periods of time. These children were essentially warehoused and left by themselves except for obligatory feedings and changing. After Ceausescu was executed in the coup of 1989, the world began to see the impact of this deprivation on young bodies and souls. On average, the children were in the third to tenth percentile for physical growth and horribly delayed in motor skills and mental development. They rocked and grasped themselves like the young monkeys in Harlow's experiments and grew up with abnormal social values and behavior. The missing ingredient in their sad lives? The blessing of loving touch.

GOD'S PLAN FOR OUR HANDS — APPROPRIATE TOUCH

Clearly, God placed enormous power in the touch of our hands, and as fathers, we must use this power to affect the young ones within our reach. I am certainly not talking about the kind of touching that seeks its own pleasure or reward. For this reason, I must add the word *appropriate* to any discussion about touch. Sadly, too many people have been touched in an inappropriate manner. God's plan for touch is pure, never self-gratifying. By his design, fathers are supposed to touch in ways that never bring any harm or discomfort to those receiving their touch. Instead, we are called to bestow the kind of touching that conveys acceptance, kindness, tenderness, and unconditional love.

We see a wonderful example of this in Mark 10:13–16. In this biblical passage, we learn that many adults were bringing their children to Jesus so that he could bless them. For reasons unknown, the disciples attempted to stop the children from getting close to Jesus. Naturally, our gentle leader reminded them that children were very much a part of the kingdom that they were seeking. Then the children came and experienced the wonderful love, gentle touch, and words of blessing from God in the flesh. According to the Scriptures, Jesus lifted the children up on his lap, put his hands on them, and blessed them. This same account is found in two other places in the Gospels, and with a bit of word study, we are able to grasp the fullest meaning of what actually happened.

To begin with, the words used to describe the young ones that came to Jesus refer to infants, toddlers, *and* half-grown boys and girls. Clearly, these were not just tiny babies that Jesus held, touched, and blessed. The phrase "laid his hands on them" is actually rooted in the Greek word *haptomai.* It means "to touch or handle something as to exert a modifying influence upon it." As we explored in the previous chapter, the final component of this scene is the blessing of words (*eulogéo*) that Jesus bestowed upon the children. Now, by putting these concepts together, we see the beauty of what really happened.

Jesus was going about his Father's business when adults began to bring their children to him to be blessed. The disciples of Jesus rejected these young people and tried to send them away, supposedly so that Jesus could get on with more important matters—whatever those were. Once this became evident, Jesus made clear that these young people did not represent a hindrance to the kingdom of God but, in fact, were precisely what God had in mind for his kingdom. The young ones came to this trusted adult, Jesus, and he brought them close to him, some even sitting on his lap. Once there, each child was touched by anointed hands in a way that caused them to feel his power, love, and acceptance. Before they left his presence, each child heard Jesus speak positive words—just for them—words that affirmed the good within them and the good awaiting them in the future.

Imagine the impact on each child who was welcomed, touched, and blessed by Jesus. These young people were truly fortunate, but with Jesus no longer walking the earth, are our own children to be denied this sort of blessing? Not if we do our part. You see, Jesus was and is our example in all things. Our character, our prayer life, our views of right and wrong, all spring from the teachings and life of Jesus Christ. However, if Christ is truly our role model, let us not stop there. We, too, must bless children, first our own and then those that have no one else to hold and bless them. In order to do so, we must move past our own fears of rejection and do as Jesus did with the children. Hold them—appropriately. Touch them—appropriately. Bless them with words that counteract the countless curses heard by every young boy or girl. Jesus did. We should, too.

A FATHER'S TOUCH

The loving words and gentle touch of a father provide incredible protection for a daughter. I am convinced that this is especially true as our girls grow into young women. However, after many years in men's ministry, I have found that fathers often withhold this sort of parental affection from their daughters just when they need it the most. Countless dads have confessed to me that they feel "strange" hugging or showing affection to their daughters after they reach puberty. This is understandable; however, we must be willing to overcome our issues to prevent our daughters from developing their own.

It should be noted that in today's society, we have many homes where girls live with stepfathers, uncles, and grandfathers who serve in the role of father. These men can certainly help to provide some of the blessing that a girl's biological father should; however, these situations must be approached very carefully. A man must always ask permission to touch any other person, even his own older daughter or stepdaughter. It is a simple yet empowering act of respect to do so. Sadly, too many of our children have been sexually and physically abused by adult men and therefore may show reluctance to any touching. As long as your motives are pure and your heart is set on blessing the young person, she will eventually allow your hand on her shoulder and ultimately a loving, paternal hug. Young people can generally sense sincerity and, with time, will open themselves up to a pure expression of fatherly love.

If you are somewhat uncomfortable with the issue of touching and hugging your own children or other young people whom God brings to you, realize that you are not alone. You may have been raised in a home where little physical affection was shown or, worse yet, in a situation where the only kind of touching that you felt was painful. However, I suggest that you seek healing for yourself so that your own pain does not cause you to withhold what others need. If you need to speak with someone about your own hurts and challenges, call a pastor, priest, or counselor so that you can become free yourself. Then, reach out to bless and encourage the young ones whom God has brought under your care. You can do it.

9

INTENTIONAL BLESSING OF A FATHER'S PRAYER

TODAY'S YOUNG WOMEN FACE CHALLENGES of many kinds. Too often, their vision, values, and virtue are under attack. As we have noted earlier in the book, it takes a systematic plan on the part of parents and other mentors to protect our daughters from these assaults. Lifelong mentoring certainly helps them make wise choices as they navigate the uncertain waters of life. Intentional blessing provides a sense of self-worth and prevents them from unnecessarily seeking the approval of others. A timely rite of passage seals the identity of each girl who experiences one of these transformational events. We fathers have been given great power with which to fight for the honor, identity, and destiny of our daughters. However, as powerful as mentoring, blessing, and rites of passage are, some issues of life are beyond their ability to reach. Fortunately, there are no issues beyond the power of prayer.

A FATHER'S CHOICE

In recent months, I have spoken with many fathers and other mentors whose daughters were facing some very difficult circumstances in life.

Some of the young women faced unwanted pregnancies, others lost jobs, and still others struggled with eating disorders. The list goes on: Disappointments over events at school. Heartless coaches who lied to the girls for their own gain. Rejection by friends. Divorce. Many of these situations were extremely complicated, and some involved people who had no interest in reconciliation or peaceful resolutions.

The fathers involved were good dads who had done their best to raise their girls. Mentoring and words of blessing were mainstays in their approach to parenting, and yet their daughters faced situations that were beyond their natural ability to influence. This meant that the men had to choose one of three options: get angry, worry, or pray. I confess that as a father, I have often chosen the first two options when my children's lives were upset by circumstances that I could not immediately "fix." More than I would like to admit, I have become angry and raged against the people involved in the situation. Sometimes I have written strong letters, made phone calls, or literally gone to address the offending parties face to face. Occasionally, these actions brought about good results. Sometimes they failed to resolve the problem at hand. Why? Because I reacted without first consulting the one who is never confused, never befuddled, and never out of options. In other words, I forgot to pray.

WHY PRAY?

As men, we often battle against problems in one of two extreme ways. Either we leap into the fray, swinging wildly until we hit something, or we pull back, hoping that things will get better by themselves. Neither approach is overly bright, especially when we have another great option so readily available to us. Why it is such a difficult option to employ is beyond me, especially since we men often pride ourselves on being so logical. Let's see...

We have the option to dive in and likely make a bad situation worse, or we can simply ask the all-powerful, omnipresent, omniscient Creator of the heavens and earth to respond to our heartfelt requests.

Okay, men. Let's take a few seconds and figure this one out. Which is the more *logical* approach? The answer is obvious but is often hidden, until we break it down into the simplest terms. At times, I really cannot explain why I still wait until I exhaust all other options (and myself) before I pray about a problem, challenge, or opportunity that affects my children. In order to be effective as a father, I must remember that many of life's challenges transcend logic and require some divine insights to overcome.

A FATHER'S PRAYER IS NEEDED DAILY

There are those who say that the answers to all of life's problems are found in the Bible. While I agree that the answers to all foundational issues are there, I do not agree that *all* of the answers to every *specific* problem or dilemma are. Here is what I mean. The Bible gives insight into vital relationships; however, it does not tell your daughter whom to date or whom to marry. The book of Proverbs provides wisdom concerning business; however, it does not instruct your daughter as to which apartment to rent, which car to buy, which of two good jobs offers to accept, and so on. The good news is that the one who gave us the precious Bible still lives today and offers to provide those answers if we only ask for them.

The book of James points this out clearly. In James 1:5 we read, "If any of you lacks wisdom, he should ask God, who gives generously to all without finding fault, and it will be given to him."

This wonderful passage of Scripture gives us the key to navigating our way out of a mess or into an opportunity. I find it fascinating that these words about prayer (asking God for wisdom *is* prayer) follow the passage instructing us to "count it all joy when we face trials." Is there a connection? Of course. God knows that trials are going to come, especially when we have the next generation to raise. However, as he has promised, he will provide the wisdom, answers, and insights that we need if we simply ask and do not doubt.

A PERSONAL EXAMPLE OF THE POWER OF PRAYER

One of the big issues that families face as their children get older is where to send them to college. So far, Kathy and I have been through this ordeal three times, with one more to go. Naturally, we did our research on each college or university under consideration and gathered as much information as possible. This process of discovery helped eliminate schools that had obvious negative aspects. In other words, we did not need help to choose between a good college and a bad college. That was easy. However, after all of the facts were considered, we still found multiple schools that offered everything that our children were looking for. The choice was between good and good. Now, we needed some divine guidance.

As parents, we recognized that the decision about which college each child would attend was incredibly important. Why? Because young people often make some of the most important choices in life during those crucial years. We knew it was likely that our children would choose their careers and perhaps even meet their future spouses during that four-year period. We needed to get this one right!

We first faced this dilemma when Jeni's oldest brother, Chris, was ready to head off to college. We narrowed it down to two excellent schools and then wrestled to make the final selection. I confess that we spent some time worrying about it, but somehow we managed to find time in our worrying to offer the situation up to God in prayer. You see, Chris not only wanted to attend a solid college but also wanted to find a school where he could fulfill his lifelong dream of playing basketball at the college level. As I look back, I can see that our prayers opened avenues that would not have otherwise been open for Chris and this vital decision. Kathy took him to visit the campus of Southeastern University in Lakeland, Florida, before the end of his senior year of high school. At that time, Chris had arranged a tryout with the coach of the basketball team and a campus tour. Kathy spent her time praying quietly as she walked around the beautiful campus, not wanting to miss any signs or clues from the Lord. As it turns out, Chris's tryout went so well that there was a possibility he would receive an offer to play for the team on the following day. So far, so good.

The beauty of prayer is that there is no distance involved, so even though Kathy and Chris were in Florida and I was in Michigan, we combined our efforts to hear from God on this key issue. The final morning that they were scheduled to be on campus, my wife and son attended a chapel service led by the president, Dr. Mark Rutland. As they entered the spacious building, filled with worshiping young people, Kathy said one last silent prayer. Unbeknownst to me, she asked the Lord for a sign that Southeastern was the school for our son. Her request was a stretch. She asked that a particular song, "Shout to the Lord," be played during worship that morning. Now, keep in mind that the chapel services at Southeastern are highly organized, and the worship team would have selected and practiced their songs well in advance of that morning's service. In other words, if they had not already picked the song, Kathy was going to be disappointed.

Well, as she tells it, the chapel service opened with prayer, which was followed by some lively praise songs played by the worship team. After several songs of praise, the leader skillfully moved the thousand or so attendees into a time of worship. My wife's thoughts were consumed with her prayer request for that certain selection to confirm our choice. After three beautiful songs, the leader announced that they would do one last number. Kathy, convinced that God was about to confirm our choice of this school for Chris, waited in wired anticipation. After a momentary pause, the worship leader's strong voice rolled across the audience, and the song he sang—you guessed it—was *not* the one that Kathy had requested of the Lord.

Now, rather than enjoy the beautiful worship song, Kathy sat down to wrestle with what to do. After all, she was not one to lightly toss out a "fleece" such as this. She truly felt that the Lord had placed it in her heart during her morning prayer to silently request that special song.

As the final musical number ended, a member of the staff approached the podium for an opening prayer. Clearly, worship was over. The musicians, now finished with their set of songs, played quietly in the background. Kathy's confidence was shaken, and she mentally began to gear up for another round of campus visitations. Suddenly, the staff member did something highly unusual. Before praying, he did an about-face, walked over to the worship leader, and whispered something in his ear. The staff member then prayed a blessing over the gathering. As he finished, the worship team broke into a thunderous rendition of—yes— "Shout to the Lord." Kathy was absolutely thrilled! It was the final, unmistakable confirmation that we needed. Chris enrolled in Southeastern as soon as he got back home.

As parents, we must understand how vital such decisions are and the role that prayer plays in making them. Upon reflection, it is easy to see that Southeastern was the right place for our oldest son. He not only made the basketball team but also was selected as a team captain in his sophomore year. That same year, his team won the national championship, setting numerous team records as well. In addition, Chris was elected student body president in his senior year. Along the way, he made lifelong friendships and learned a great deal about himself, his world, and the God who created it all. Could any of this have happened at another school? Perhaps, but probably not. Through prayer, God's will for our son was determined, and this young man was launched into his future and his destiny. Through prayer.

YOUR TURN TO PRAY

Fathers, mothers, mentors, please commit to pray for the women, young and old, in your lives. They need our daily prayers much more than they need our worry. When we pray, we commit them into the hands of their heavenly Father and place them under his loving care. That is the ultimate intentional blessing.

OUR PLAN FOR OUR DAUGHTERS is now really taking shape. We have learned how important it is to mentor and teach them about life, character, and integrity. In addition, we discovered the amazing impact that our positive words, touch, and prayer can have. Next, we need to help our daughters make the transition from girlhood to womanhood. This can be accomplished through a powerful ceremony or rite of passage that is held during her teen years.

PART 3

❧

FOUNDATIONS
FOR
CELEBRATIONS

10

A GIRL'S RITE OF PASSAGE; WHY IT MATTERS

ALL GIRLS WANT TO KNOW "When do I become a woman?" All boys want to know "When do I become a man?" A rite of passage answers those questions once and for all. Here is why.

A "rite of passage" is a ceremony or event in which respected elders bestow the status of adulthood upon a young person. It marks the transition from childhood to adulthood.

I have had many years to ponder the impact that rites of passage hold for today's youth. Initially, I questioned whether a rite of passage would actually help young males or females make the transition into mature adulthood. Now, after participating in countless ceremonies and seeing their impact on both those being celebrated and those in attendance, my question has changed from "Will it work?" to *Why* does it work?"

Today, after more than a decade of studying this powerful concept, I understand at least some of the reasons why rites of passage are so effective in young people's lives. Foundationally, rites of passage work because they answer the one question—"When?"—that every young person needs to have answered.

In reality, the answer to the question is simple and yet profound: girls become women and boys become men *when the elders of their family and/or broader society declare them so.*

This powerful truth has been well understood by many other cultures for countless generations. The following story about a Navajo girl's transition into adulthood is just one example of how powerful a rite of passage can be.

KINAALDA — ONE GIRL'S PASSAGE

Celeste's raven-black hair flies as she runs, and small puffs of red dust leap into the air with each step. Although tired from lack of sleep and sore from her ordeal, the young woman's stride remains strong. Today is the final day of her coming-of-age celebration. This rite-of-passage ceremony, called Kinaalda, began four days earlier and will soon be over. Each day Celeste has had to run farther and faster than the day before, always toward the life-giving sun.

Celeste was considered a girl when she began this final run, but from the moment she crosses the finish line, she will be forevermore received as a woman by the members of her tribe. This young woman has always been proud of her Native-American heritage, but never more so than today. As she runs, Celeste thinks of the many relatives who have gathered on the reservation in New Mexico to be part of her Kinaalda.

In her mind, Celeste reminisces about the events of the past few days:

My Kinaalda began when I first entered into the hut, where my mother and aunts helped me to prepare. First, they brushed my hair with a special brush of grass stems and tied it with a buckskin cord. Then, my family sang the first of many prayers. The initial prayer was sung for nearly thirty minutes, others lasted well over an hour. On that first morning, I changed into a beautiful black-and-red dress that my aunt made for me. Silver concho shells had been stitched onto the edges. Mother then placed a heavy turquoise necklace around my neck, and I laced the buckskin moccasins all the way up my calves. All of this was just the beginning of my Kinaalda, my Blessing Way.

Next, the medicine man instructed my mother to "mold" me into the woman that I am to become by placing her hands on my head, stomach, eyes, and feet. Then, many people actually came before me so that I could touch them! I could feel the power in my hands as I stroked little babies and even aging grandmothers. Truly, the Great Spirit was there. After the molding was finished, I went for my first run of the day. I flew out of the hogan and headed east, where each day begins, followed by many of my family and friends. On the initial run, I went over a half mile before turning around and returning. I was so excited! And now...I am nearly finished!

In support of her quest, Celeste's grandparents, father, mother, aunts, uncles, and many friends all set aside several days to show their love. In fact, since it began, more than forty people have taken part in her special ceremony. They all worked so hard, especially her close relatives, to cook, clean, and pray, just for her.

Each day of her Kinaalda, Celeste prays, works, and runs. In preparation for her final day, she began one of the most important aspects of her rite-of-passage ceremony: baking a huge cake in the earth. This may sound like a small matter; however, this is no ordinary cake! It is baked in a hole dug in the sand that is four feet across and nearly a foot deep. The ingredients are cornmeal, the staple of her people, as well as hot water and a sweetener. The elaborate process is fascinating. First, a wood fire is made in the hole to sear the sand with intense heat. Next, the cake batter is prepared by hand. This means that Celeste must stir the batter for nearly an hour before it is ready for baking. Then the young woman sews cornhusks together to make two crust-covers for the cake. Her first attempts fail; she is both scolded and encouraged by the female relatives watching her every move. After hours of work, she finally puts the cake batter into the hole for baking. Much symbolism accompanies this important step. Celeste is instructed to sprinkle cornmeal on top of the cake as a blessing. The other people gathered for her Kinaalda follow her example and sprinkle the cake with cornmeal. Next, the cake is covered, and a fire is built on top of it so that it cooks until the following morning. If all goes well, it will be eaten after her final run.

Once the cake is placed in the ground, Celeste returns to the hogan for a night of praying. She must stay awake until dawn to receive the blessing of the prayers. Each sacred saying will introduce her to the Holy People who watch over the Navajos and will ask the Great Spirit to protect her on her journey through life. She is joined in the hogan by the medicine man and many other adults who will help pray during the night. From dark until dawn, Celeste must sit with her legs stretched out in front of her and her back straight. Her pain is eased by the beautiful chorus coming from the family members who surround her on this sacred evening.

Shortly before dawn, her final run begins. Family and friends grow quiet as the blanket covering the hogan door is thrown back, letting in the first rays of the sun. Celeste leaps from the hogan and runs the mysterious race during which this girl transforms into a woman. She runs fast—faster and farther than ever before. Strengthened by the prayers and support of her family, she flies down the dusty road toward the awakening dawn.

I am almost finished, Celeste says to herself. *My time as a little girl is nearly over. I am ready to move into this new season of my life!*

When Celeste returns she is tired but happy. Quickly she walks to where her cake has been baking all night and removes the covering. Her mother cuts into the beautiful creation and announces that it is perfectly cooked. Celeste is relieved. Anything less would be a bad sign.

Only two tasks remain in her rite-of-passage ceremony. Once again, people come before Celeste so that she can lay her hands upon them for a time of blessing. Then the cake is cut into pieces and offered to her friends and family. The center pieces are reserved for special guests such as her grandmother and the medicine man.

Soon the cake is eaten, and her ceremony draws to a peaceful close. The young Navajo woman now rests before making her way home. Her joy is uncontainable. The young girl has finished her race. Celeste is now a woman.

OUR MODERN DILEMMA

The Kinaalda ceremony is powerful evidence that traditional Navajo parents understand what many in our modern society have forgotten—or never knew to begin with. That is, when a culture chooses to set a strategic course, its children become adults by design rather than by default. Certainly, the Navajos are not the only culture to implement strategies for the transformation of their daughters into productive adults. For example, the Jewish culture has a coming-of-age ceremony called Bat Mitzvah. These rites-of-passage events are conducted with reverence, honoring the traditions of the Jewish people and welcoming their daughters into womanhood. Other ceremonies, held in faraway jungles, push girls to their physical limits as a means of signifying that a transition into adulthood has occurred. The results of these events are powerful and compelling. Of course, it is important to realize that the cultures that most effectively utilize rites of passage also invest significant time in their girls prior to the special event. Concerned adults provide training, mentoring, correction, words of blessing, and more to prepare their daughters for a time of transition. However, whether a rite of passage involves tests of endurance, increased spiritual insights, or personal deprivation, each produces a near-miraculous outcome. When the event is over, a girl becomes a woman, better prepared to accept new responsibilities and to walk boldly into her destiny.

In sharp contrast, our modern, supposedly advanced society is essentially devoid of any such ceremonies for our daughters. We content ourselves with the notion that somehow adulthood just happens with the passing of time. What a mistake. Children transition into adulthood best when the adults of their societies welcome them in through powerful transitional events. In those cultures, young males and females accept their parents' and other elders' declarations about adulthood as truth. As soon as they reach the appropriate age and participate in their rite-of-passage ceremonies, the young people are accepted as adults. Immediately afterward, they *begin* to live according to the new adult expectations. I stress the word *begin* here for a very important reason. There is a difference between adulthood and maturity.

ADULTHOOD VS. MATURITY

While a modern rite of passage instantly bestows the designation of man or woman upon the young celebrant, along with some new responsibilities and freedoms, it does not make them instantly mature. This takes time, training, education, and more. For this reason, I do not advocate that we lower the legal age for certain activities such as driving, drinking, voting, serving in the military, or getting married. Many young people are simply not ready to handle such things without a great deal of counsel, mentoring, and support from others. However, this is not because they have not yet reached manhood or womanhood; rather, it is because they are not yet *mature.*

We must realize that young people today need adults to simply and confidently answer their questions about growing up and then take them through the door to adulthood. A rite-of-passage celebration, hosted by a loving parent and/or other mentors, is the one event that will mark that special day of transition from childhood to adulthood. That one special day will forever answer all the questions about "when?" for any child. From that day on, the question in the mind of a young person will focus on how to act like an adult rather than on when he or she will become one.

THE CORNERSTONE OF WOMANHOOD

I am convinced that a rite-of-passage celebration leads to mature adulthood just as, in orthodox Christian teaching, salvation leads to sanctification. Here is why. A person becomes a Christian at the moment he or she accepts Christ by faith and is thereby born anew spiritually. This person's rightful position and identity is as a full-fledged member of God's family. The person can never be more of a Christian than at the moment of acceptance. He or she will become much more spiritually *mature*, but not more of a Christian. Scripture does not teach that we earn our Christianity by degrees, levels, or ages. It teaches that acceptance of Christ is the door through which one enters into the faith and is fully accepted into the fold.

Naturally, the new convert must be taught what the works of a mature Christian are and how to do them. These works include a renewal of the mind and heart, which leads to changes in one's attitudes, behaviors, communication, and worldview. Clearly each new believer goes through a process of maturity; however, before any maturing takes place, new converts must first accept that a miraculous transformation has occurred. They must first acknowledge that they have transitioned from one state or condition into another totally different one.

In like manner, a young person must first accept the fact that he or she *is* an adult before it ever makes sense for them to do the *works* of a mature adult. Obviously, a teenager is not fully developed physically, mentally, emotionally, or spiritually. However, at a rite of passage, the individual is formally and publicly welcomed into adulthood. From loving elders, the celebrant learns that he or she was created by God to grow into maturity and that there are specific good works that have been prepared in advance to do (see Ephesians 2:8–10). Once the parents and other elders formally declare that the child has become an adult, the child is then positioned to experience a miraculous change. From that moment on, the goal becomes a very reachable one of increasing levels of maturity rather than the impossible goal of self-appointed adulthood. In this way, the rite of passage acts as the door into adulthood, just as salvation is the door to sanctification and maturity for a believer.

On the other hand, if young males or females never walk through the door to adulthood, they are then condemned to wander for years outside of their intended domain. Confused and questioning, the teens stumble into an uncertain future by default rather than boldly pursuing it by design with the help of mature elders. Without a transitional event to mark the passage into adulthood, the young people will literally spend many years trying to discover ways to confirm their own coming of age. Sadly, they always look for a random *action* rather than for a sanctioned *event* to mark this transition. Our young people today are vainly substituting their first cigarette, drink, sexual encounter, theft, or some other mile marker for true transitional events. Are so-called good kids protected from such folly? Not at all. While they may avoid some of the more sensational practices, they often chase their adulthood in perfectionism, overworking, and striving for the best grades in school and yet never really feel satisfied in who they are. It is infinitely better for mature adults to lead our young people into role-defining rites of passage. These rites really work. Now let's examine exactly how they work in our modern-day society.

11

PREPARATION FOR JENI'S RITE OF PASSAGE

AS KATHY AND I PLANNED for Jenifer's rite of passage, I could not help but reflect upon our older sons' events that took place years earlier. There was a flood of memories associated with Christopher's and Steven's celebrations. Most of it was good; however, there is a bitter-sweet element to any rite of passage. Let me explain.

When we acknowledge that our children are growing up, we must also accept the fact that *we* are growing older. Transitions rarely affect only one member of a family, and with each rite of passage in the Molitor home, my heart was tested. I often feel that time has become my enemy as I watch my children grow. With each passing day, my children transform more and more, seeming to change right before my eyes. I am truly torn by this reality.

As a father, I had to accept the fact that the day would come when I had to release my children into their own futures. Nevertheless, part of me always wanted to keep them as little ones forever. I wrestled with the notion that the toddlers who once climbed on my lap, begging me to read a storybook for the twentieth time, soon had other things to do.

At times, I still selfishly wish life could be made up of endless summers spent swimming or playing with them. That is my wish; however, it has never been God's plan. Eventually, I came to realize that if I did not help my children to mature, I risked losing them to lifestyles of childishness that would ultimately destroy them and our relationship. It is a painful reality, but to prepare and then release a child is a father's duty.

LAYING THE FOUNDATIONS

One of the most interesting decisions Kathy and I had to make when we planned our first rite of passage was what to call it. To call it a *party* sounded too trite. Moreover, the term *ceremony* made it sound as if the attendees would need to dress in flowing saffron robes and chant just to get in the door. We finally settled on the term *celebration* as the most appropriate. After all, that is the whole point of the event: to celebrate a son's or daughter's transition from childhood into adulthood.

Once we knew what to call the event, we then determined its fundamental components. Kathy and I concluded that, just as with the boys' rites of passage, three key ingredients were needed for Jeni's celebration: a sharing of wisdom from special mentors, life lessons in the form of skits, and a time of spiritual blessing.

Developing the time of blessing

Without question, Kathy and I wanted the celebration to have a strong spiritual foundation. Early in the planning stage, we were reminded of a biblical account of blessing and celebration that really touched us. It gave us a good idea of what to include during the blessing portion of Jeni's celebration. The passage recounts our heavenly Father's blessing of his Son. As I stated earlier, there is no difference between male and female when it comes to God's principles, practices, and especially his blessings. Just as this passage provided direction for our sons' rites of passage, we knew that we could utilize it as a guide for Jeni's.

A CHILD BELOVED:
PRONOUNCING A FATHER'S PLEASURE

The biblical account of blessing that we used as a pattern for Jenifer's celebration is found in Matthew 3:16–17. It records the events that took place when Jesus was baptized in the river Jordan and the Holy Spirit descended on him. As Jesus rose out of the water, his heavenly Father declared from heaven, "This is my Son, whom I love; with him I am well pleased." Later it is recorded that on the Mount of Transfiguration, the heavenly Father once again said, "This is my Son, whom I love; with him I am well pleased" (Matt. 17:5).

How significant that the Father said, *"This* is my Son." If Jesus in his humanity doubted his divine heritage for even a moment, these few words confirming his sonship would have put those doubts to rest. However, if this were his Father's only purpose, he would have said, *"You* are my beloved Son," addressing Jesus alone. By saying *"This* is my Son," the heavenly Father served notice to all creation that the promised, divine Savior had arrived. He let every being in the universe know who this man was and how his Father felt about him.

Ironically, or perhaps predictably, just a short time after this wonderful blessing was spoken, this beloved Son was assaulted by the varied schemes of Satan. In Matthew 4:1–11 we see the devil tempt Jesus to turn stones into bread, to test the Father's love by casting himself down from a high tower, and to worship the deceiver in exchange for all the world's kingdoms. Jesus, however, rejects all three temptations, realizing they are but smoke screens for Satan's real objective: to separate Jesus from the blessing, purpose, and identity that his Father has recently bestowed on him. This is why Satan begins two of his seductive statements to Jesus with the words, *"If* you are the Son of God."

If Satan had somehow managed to confuse Jesus about his true identity or convince him that he was not the Son of God, the course of human history would have been dramatically altered. Instead, Jesus believed his Father, received his identity, and dutifully carried out his heaven-sent mission on earth.

After studying this Bible passage, we were convinced that our celebration for Jenifer needed to include a spoken blessing, confirmation of her identity, and a declaration of just how pleased both Kathy and I were with her as our daughter.

PRESSING AHEAD

Just as every child is unique, so should be his or her celebration. One child will do better if just a few people are in attendance. Another will thrive with a whole room full of attendees. One child will respond well to skits, while another will learn more from the presentation of a simple, short message. These events are not "one size fits all." Each must be designed with the individual child in mind. It is good to explore all options and alternatives before making any final decisions about who should attend, what should be taught, and what format should be followed. Kathy and I eventually decided upon the people and events that would make up Jeni's special day. I have asked Kathy to share from her perspective what went into the planning process. Her insights are priceless for the mother or female mentor who will coordinate the celebration for her daughter.

MOTHER'S DUTIES

Kathy here...

The very first thing we needed to establish was the date for Jeni's celebration. We settled on Saturday, September 7, knowing that six weeks would give us enough time to prepare for her big day. Brian had held the boys' celebrations at one of the local hotels. That had worked well, but I decided to hold Jenifer's event at a different hotel—one that could offer us those little extras that a girl like Jeni would appreciate. I made an appointment to meet with the events coordinator at the hotel, and from this meeting, the plans for our celebration began to take shape. I was able to establish the size of the room, the setup for the tables and podium, and what refreshments we would have. Driving home from the hotel that day, my mind was filled with a thousand questions. Whom should we invite? How could I make this extra-special for Jeni? Most important, what life lessons did God want to impart to our precious daughter?

Brian and I began to prayerfully consider who should attend Jeni's rite-of-passage celebration. We began with Jeni's grandmothers and some close family friends. The key was to invite women who were spiritually and emotionally mature. Once the list was completed, I wrote the following letter to each woman:

Dear Ladies,

It has been five years since we first celebrated the rite of passage of our eldest son, Chris. Since that time, we have honored Steven with his own celebration and have seen the impact these special events have had on both of them, as well as on many

other young men and women—those with whom we ha
sonally celebrated and others we have heard about in r
to Brian's book *Boy's Passage*. Little did we know in 1
that God had planned to do in using Chris's celebration to birth
a book, which in turn has been a catalyst to help many other sons
and daughters in their journeys toward maturity by celebrating their own rites of passage.

Now the time has come for Brian and me to honor another
one of our own children—this time our precious daughter,
Jenifer. She is now thirteen, and we have watched her grow from
a sweet, little girl into a lovely, young woman. It is truly a pleasure to hold this special celebration to honor and affirm her as
a young woman and her role as a daughter of the King for such
a time as this.

We request the honor of your presence
at the Rite of Passage Celebration
for our beloved daughter, Jenifer Elizabeth,
to be held on Saturday, September 7, 2002
beginning at 7:00 pm
_____ Hotel
Midland, Michigan

In order to make this event a meaningful one, we truly hope
that you will be able to attend. We also need your help in a few
different ways. We covet your prayers for Jeni over the next few
weeks: that God's anointing would be on this celebration and
that her heart and mind would be touched. We also ask that you
write a letter to Jeni that you will bring with you on the 7th,
or you may send it before her celebration if you are unable to
attend. Words have such power to build up and to minister.
Perhaps you have a life lesson, a scripture, a nugget of wisdom
you could share, or a word of encouragement for her as she grows
into all that God has planned for her life. Lastly, would you
please bring a small, symbolic gift—something that she can
treasure to remind her of this special night as we reach out to
express our love for her and to bless this precious young lady?

If you are unable to attend but wish to send a letter or small gift, it may be sent to our home address, or you may email us.

Thank you for helping us bless our daughter at this special time in her life.

Sincerely and with love,

Kathy Molitor

I confess that I struggled a little the day I dropped the invitations off at the post office. Now I was committed! So many insecure thoughts whirled in my mind. I knew how powerful the boys' rites of passage had been. But this time it was up to me; Brian wouldn't be leading the event. What if it didn't turn out as well as theirs? What if most of the ladies couldn't come, or if the skits didn't make sense? What I really needed to understand was that it wasn't about me. My primary role was to seek God in prayer, gather other women around me for support, and trust God that he would grace us with his presence and would place his anointing on the event, because it was his desire to bless our—no, his—daughter Jeni.

During the preparation phase, I asked three of my close friends to help me with the celebration. I found this to be invaluable. Not only did they have insightful ideas to share, but they were always there to encourage me. God used their unique gifts and talents to make the entire celebration a success.

I chose my dear friend Ann to be the mistress of ceremonies for the celebration. Ann has known Jeni since she was four years old and loves her like a daughter. Besides, she has the gift of organization, is given to detail, and is very gracious. My job was to provide her with the master agenda and with a detailed outline to guide her, and I knew she would do well. Another one of my good friends, Heidi, agreed to help me with the skits. Heidi's ever-present hunger for the Word and her gift of teaching made her the ideal person to do the mini-teachings that would both precede and follow the skits. These would be the life lessons, meant to impart wisdom and encouragement, in particular to Jeni, but also to each woman present.

Now we were getting to the most challenging part of this whole planning phase. I wanted...no, I needed to hear from God about the life lessons he wanted Jeni to learn. So we earnestly prayed for guidance and wisdom. Once the concepts were established, we began to focus on the scriptures, the key points to each teaching, and the planning of the skits themselves. Heidi and I worked on the teachings together. She has four children, too, and so it wasn't always easy scheduling time together. I remember one afternoon when she met me at the nail salon. We sat for an hour, Bibles on our laps, taking notes and going over each teaching. It was not the most spiritual setting, but it worked!

As part of the planning process, I asked a family friend, Catherine, who was visiting from Trinidad, if she would be willing to select a song to sing during the celebration. She has such a beautiful voice and a sweet spirit, and she lovingly agreed to do so. Last but not least, I asked two of Jeni's friends to serve as greeters at the door of our meeting room. Their role was to hand each woman the program I'd prepared, help with the name tags, and receive any gifts that our guests had brought. This allowed me to mingle with the women who had already arrived.

Everything seemed to be in place with the help and support of my friends, with Brian's encouragement, and with God's grace and guidance. I knew with this team effort and with God in control, Jeni's evening would be everything we had hoped for—and it was!

PART 4

ONE DAUGHTER'S STORY

12

LET THE
CELEBRATION
BEGIN!

AS WE SHARE JENI'S SPECIAL EVENING with you, please know that this is an example, not a formula. Your resources, budget, creativity, and family "style" all play into the planning of this time. It can be a simple affair or more complex, whichever you choose. Feel free to tailor-make this event for your young woman who is like no other on the planet. Here is Jeni's story.

Brian here...

A week before her rite of passage, I asked Jeni if she would allow me to escort her to a nice restaurant for dinner on the evening of her celebration. Thankfully, she accepted, and I set about making plans for the last meal that I would ever share with my little girl. Now, Dad, if you think that I was going to get emotional about such an event...you are right.

When the special evening finally came, I shined my shoes, cleaned out my car, and dressed up in my best suit. Hey, I definitely wanted to impress my date! Kathy agreed to help get Jenifer ready, not only for our dinner date but also for her celebration that would follow. A little after five o'clock, Jeni came down the stairs accompanied by her mother.

They both walked into the family room where I waited patiently. (Okay, not patiently, but at least I waited.) My daughter was a remarkable sight. The little girl who just hours before was dressed in jeans and a tee shirt had been completely transformed under Kathy's watchful eye. Despite the fact that she was just fourteen years of age, Jenifer could have easily passed for a young woman at least five years older. Her honey-blonde hair was beautifully pulled up and stood out against the striking black dress that Mom helped select for this special night. With a deep sense of ceremony, I presented my daughter with an orchid corsage, placing it upon her wrist. Next, we took several photos and then headed to the restaurant, which was located in the conference center where later that evening Jeni's rite of passage would be held.

Upon arrival, we found the setting to be perfect for such a special date between a father and his daughter. Freshly starched linen table-cloths, neatly folded napkins, and the full array of silverware graced the table, which sat in a quiet corner of the room. Jeni and I placed our orders and began to talk about this time of transition that was taking place. As usual, I was impressed by my daughter's maturity. Her words have always been weighty, and there is a God-given depth to her thoughts.

A couple of times she caught me staring at her and tearing up during the course of the meal. I knew that this impressive young woman was ready to make the transition, and I was thankful that God had chosen me to be her father. She just smiled and gracefully allowed me to be a softhearted dad. That night I ate slowly, not wanting the meal to end.

Just before dessert, I told Jenifer that I had a special surprise for her. Jeni's eyes sparkled as I pulled a small, velvet box from my suit pocket and set it on the table in front of her. The conversation went something like this...

"Okay, Dad, what's in the box?"

"Well, Jen, it's something special. Just for you."

"Can I open it?"

"Not yet. Let me explain... Have you ever heard of a promise ring?" I asked.

She nodded.

"Well, this is similar, but there is a big difference. A promise ring is usually a ring that a young person chooses to wear as a symbol of a promise to God, their parents, and themselves that they will remain sexually pure until their wedding day," I explained as I handed her the box. "Go ahead, honey. Open it and I will tell you more…"

Jeni slowly lifted the top of the box to reveal a beautiful ring that Kathy and I had selected. The bright blue stone sparkled in the candlelight and reflected the smile on Jenifer's face. I continued with my explanation.

"Here is the difference. This ring comes with a promise too. Except in this case, *I* am the one making the promise. You see, since the moment you were conceived, God's plan was for me to be the man in your life, at least for the first couple of decades. As such, I have been and will continue to be your protector, your provider, your counselor, your covering, and so much more. No man on the face of the earth loves you as much or as sincerely as I do. Honey, I would give my life for you."

The words were getting harder to say, and I wrestled to keep my composure. Somehow I stumbled and bumbled my way through the remainder of my thoughts.

"Jeni, I want you to know that if there is anything that you need, I will do all that I can to provide it for you. You can stay with your mom and me for as long as you want, and as God's plan becomes clear for your own destiny, I will help you to achieve it. So, during this time, please wear this ring as a symbol of my promise to be the man in your life. I am your father, and to love you in this way is my honor, my privilege, my joy, and my duty."

Yes, sir, it was really tough at that point, but I continued anyway.

"Honey, when the day comes that God brings another man into your life, the one who will be your husband, I will gladly step to the side and allow him to walk with you into your destiny. And…on your wedding day, when you take him to be your husband, you can choose to keep this ring…or you can give it back to your old dad."

That moment remains frozen in time for me. I recall Jenifer's beautiful smile and my promise ring shining on her finger. Most of all, I remember a feeling deep within my own heart of incredible love for my daughter. The kind of love that mirrors our heavenly Father's love for his children. Pure. Unselfish. Outward-focused with no concern that anything be given in return. It is different from a man's love for his wife. It is different from a father's love for his sons. It is incredibly unique. A father's love for his daughter. What a marvelous feeling for a father to have.

After sitting quietly for so long and listening to her dad's tearful talk, Jenifer's response was perfect.

"Thanks, Daddy. I will always keep it."

Soon, too soon, it was time to take Jeni on my arm and walk to the meeting room where her mother and her destiny waited patiently for her arrival.

THE GUEST OF HONOR ARRIVES

Kathy here...

September 7 finally arrived and with it much anticipation and excitement. There were several phone calls to make to my "helpers" to confirm our plans. I always have lists to get me through normal days, but since this one was special, my list was longer than usual. I had the cake to pick up and deliver to the hotel. Check. All the props for the skits to take with me. Check. Mustn't forget Jeni's wrapped gift. Check. Stop to get Jeni's corsage. Check. Soon it was time for me to get dressed for the occasion.

As soon as Jeni left for her date with Brian, I jumped into my car and headed to the hotel to set up. There was much to be done before the guests arrived, but I was mercifully greeted at our meeting room by my trusted friends Ann, Heidi, and Shaenon. Together, we put everything in its place, went over the agenda, and then joined hands to pray one last time before the other ladies arrived.

Jeni's grandmothers were the first to enter. Then, one by one, the others walked through the door and into Jeni's special night. It was such a joy to know that these women had taken the time to come and bless our daughter. I was thrilled to have each one there: twenty-three in all.

The hotel staff served us coffee and punch, and soon the room was filled with laughter, smiles, and warm conversation as we waited for Jeni to arrive. Soft worship music filled the air, a gentle reminder of what the evening was all about.

One of the girls kept an eye on the hallway leading from the restaurant as Jeni's anticipated time of arrival neared. Excitedly, she whispered to me that Jeni was about to arrive. With microphone in hand, Ann announced Jeni's arrival just as her father escorted her through the door. I don't know which one was smiling more—Jeni or her proud dad, presenting his beloved daughter to the elders who had gathered. I can still hear the cheers and clapping as our guest of honor appeared at the entrance. From the look on her face, I could tell that Jenifer was filled with a sense of wonder and joy.

Jeni was welcomed by many of the women as she made her way across the room to the collage that I had created for her out of photos from her childhood. After a time of fellowship and refreshments, Ann called us all to sit down so that the ceremony could begin. We asked each woman to introduce herself and tell the group what her relationship was to Jeni or our family. Since many of the ladies did not know one another, it was interesting to learn what brought each of them together for such an important event. After the introductions, Ann opened our time together in prayer and then called Heidi and Shaenon to the front of the room. It was time to introduce the skits and to experience their powerful messages.

13

LESSONS
FOR LIFE

HEIDI INTRODUCED THE FIRST SKIT by reading a key scripture from Romans 12:6: "We have different gifts, according to the grace given us."

She then read a portion from 1 Corinthians 12:14–25, which talks about the body being made up of many parts. Paraphrasing, it tells of how one part is no less important than the other parts. That each part is needed.

Heidi continued reading: "But in fact, God has arranged the parts in the body, every one of them, just as he wanted them to be. If they were all one part, where would the body be?"

SKIT #1: IF ONLY I COULD BE...

With these verses in mind, Heidi asked Shaenon to begin a skit that we called "If Only I Could Be..."

The lights were dimmed as a large wall divider and table were pushed to the front of the room. Hanging on the divider were three distinctly different clothing outfits. Appropriate accessories had been placed on the table in front of each one. Shaenon had positioned herself out of sight, behind the divider. This gave the illusion that the outfits themselves were talking, and by using a different accent and speaking style, each outfit took on a character of its own.

A bright light was directed toward a beautiful blue evening gown appropriately named "Lady Glamour." In front of "her" were a pair of high-heeled sandals, an evening bag, and rhinestone necklace and earrings. Speaking in a slow, sultry voice, Lady Glamour began to compare her "life" to the other two characters, symbolized by the outfits. She imagined how much better life would be if she could be "Miss Athlete," who had all the fun and who had fans cheering and clapping whenever she was around. Next, she compared herself to "Ms. Professional," imagining what it would be like to be taken seriously, to have people interested in what you have to say. If only she could be like them...

Just then, Ms. Professional spoke up as the spotlight revealed a professional looking two-piece suit hanging in front of a briefcase and a pair of pumps.

Her voice sounded very prim and proper, as she began to comment about what Lady Glamour had to say. Ms. Professional complained that all she ever did was work and was upset that no one ever noticed her, except for her brains. She envied the fact that Lady Glamour could go to fancy dinner parties and spend the evening dancing and that Miss Athlete could get trophies and medals for her accomplishments—when all she ever got was more paperwork. Oh, if only she could be like Lady Glamour and Miss Athlete.

Next, Miss Athlete began to speak, breathless and tired from her daily workout.

The spotlight shone on a basketball uniform, a basketball, a water bottle, and athletic shoes. With her quick, youthful, upbeat voice, she began to imagine how wonderful it would be to have the career of Ms. Professional or to be treated like a princess, as was Lady Glamour.

At this point, the ceiling lights came on, and Heidi moved toward the podium. She began to address what had just taken place before our very eyes. The room was still as she took us to God's Word:

"For you created my inmost being; you knit me together in my mother's womb. I praise you because I am fearfully and wonderfully made; your works are wonderful, I know that full well." Psalm 139:13–14.

Heidi explained that each of us has unique gifts and talents, given to us by God. She taught us that no one gift is more important than another—though they may be different. Also that we should not be envious of another's gift or talent but rather be content with what God has given us, for He has "fearfully and wonderfully made" each of us.

Once again the lights dimmed and the spotlight rested on Ms. Professional.

She had taken time to think about who she was and what her role was in this life. Her perspective had changed, and she began talking about what great opportunities she had to change the world through her profession. So considering everything, she came to the conclusion that she was happy being who God had made her to be.

Our attention then turned to Miss Athlete, who began to talk to herself. She recollected how exciting it was to be a part of the basketball team. She talked about the crowds cheering and that she would be bored with anything else. She realized how much fun her life was and how much she loved the game of basketball.

At last, it was Lady Glamour's turn, and all eyes were now on the gorgeous royal blue gown. She began to describe how thrilling it was to tango or waltz across a dance floor and how exciting it was when her necklace sparkled in just the right light. She said how thankful she was that God had gifted her with such a life.

With that, Heidi once again stood to summarize the skit. The message was clear. Each had compared her own life to the other characters, wishing she could be someone other than who she was. Each was initially envious of the others—not realizing that who she was made to be was just fine. In the end, each came to a place of contentment with her own identity and with the destiny that God had planned for her.

SKIT #2: MIRROR, MIRROR ON THE WALL

Heidi introduced the second skit by asking the group a rhetorical question: "How many of you wish you could be different?" She warned us of the enemy's plan to destroy our self-esteem and that he often uses other people to say hurtful things to us. She also talked about the Hollywood standards that we are bombarded with daily: the Barbie-doll figures, the blemish-free faces, and pictures on magazines airbrushed to perfection. These images feed into the unrealistic expectations to be prettier, thinner, taller, shapelier, and so on.

With this to ponder, Heidi asked Shaenon to come to the front.
Now, Shaenon is a pretty, young woman with brown eyes, long hair, and
an attractive figure. There was only one thing she did to prepare herself for this skit—it was to use a dark marker to draw numerous large
freckles across the bridge of her nose and her cheeks.

The skit began with Shaenon standing in front of a full-length mirror, readying herself for a party. Looking into the mirror at her own
reflection, she began to criticize what she saw. She did not like her com-
plexion, her hair, or her figure, for that matter. After all, she had freckles on her face, and she did not like the shape of her nose. Turning
sideways, she began complaining to herself about how fat she was.
Obviously troubled, discouraged, and frustrated, she sank down into the
blue chair that had been placed next to the mirror. Maybe she would
not even go the party.

Suddenly, a deep male voice could be heard from the back of the
room, as I quietly turned on the tape player. It was God (actually it was
Brian on tape...) calling Shaenon by name, saying that He wanted to
talk with her. At first she wondered if God would actually want to talk
with her. Her doubts were evident. However, as she began to listen
intently, Brian's voice could be heard speaking in a caring, tender way,
much as I imagine our Father God himself would speak to his precious
daughter. This is what "God" said:

> Well of course it is me. You know I'm always with you. Tonight
> I was noticing that you spent a long time in front of that mirror.
> From the look on your face and the heaviness I sense in your heart,
> it tells me we need to have a little talk. A talk about beauty.
>
> My precious daughter, there is outer beauty and there is
> inner beauty. The outer beauty, well, that changes. It changes
> with the seasons, it changes with what society says it is, and
> Hollywood, television, and magazines—they all try to create
> something different with each new season, for beauty. Some-
> times it's a different color of hair, and sometimes its fashion
> and make-up. I know my precious daughters are constantly
> bombarded with images of what outer beauty should really be.
> This has gone on through the centuries, and there have been
> whole societies that have thought that the bigger a woman was,
> the more beautiful and attractive she was. Other societies have

thought that the smallest women were the most attractive, and the ones with the tiniest little waists were the most beautiful. Well, it amuses me to watch this go on and to watch societies try in so many different ways to create a beautiful outside, when all they really need to do is to allow me to create a beautiful inside—for them to be truly beautiful.

Now you my daughter, your inner beauty cannot help but come out because I have made you in my own image—and I am love, and I have placed love within you. I see that love that is so deep within you, and it comes out when you see children and animals. You are a loving person, daughter. That is part of that inner beauty I have placed in you. You are kind and gentle, and those too, make up parts of the inner beauty of you. I have placed within you the fruit of my Spirit, and that helps to make you beautiful, as well. You are patient and gentle. You have self-control, but daughter, tonight, I sense that you have lost two of those fruits. They have fallen from your basket. Joy and peace escape you when you focus too much on that outer beauty—the reflection you see in the mirror. Tonight I want you to allow me to place within you greater measures of joy and peace as you rest in the truth that your Father has made you unique and special. As the Creator of the universe, I could have made everyone exactly the same, but there is no beauty in that. I delight to see differences in my children. I have caused you to show different aspects of your Creator. I call that beautiful.

So tonight I invite you to stand up and look again at what you see. Those things that you see as flaws—consider them to be my special touches on your life. And by the way, those freckles—you seem to want to get rid of them. I painted each one by hand, just so I could touch your face. You are my precious daughter, and the beauty that resides within you is so much greater than anything that could be seen on the outside. That outer beauty—it can fade, and over the years it changes. But the beauty I have placed within you will never change. In fact, it increases as years go by and you grow to know me better.

So, daughter, stand up. Look once more in that mirror and tell me what you see. See the inner beauty I have placed within you. Tonight as we go, let's go together. I would be honored to take your arm, daughter, and walk you into any room as your beauty shines from the inside. For you are the apple of my eye, and I greatly delight in you.

The room was so very quiet. I believe each woman there, at one time or another, had been like the character that Shaenon played—discontent with her own appearance, feeling ugly, or fat, or maybe too skinny. What the heavenly Father had spoken to his daughter was what every woman there needed to hear to counter the endless lies aimed at destroying the self-esteem of God's daughters. While I know it was meant for Jeni, I also sensed in my spirit that God was ministering to each of us in a very personal way.

When the taped message had finished, Shaenon stood up from her chair and looked into the mirror again. This time, a look of disgust was replaced with a gentle smile. She straightened her sweater, combed her hair once more as she readied to leave for the party—this time with the Lord at her side, encouraging her all the way.

With this, Heidi rose from her chair and walked to the front of the room. She read the following verses from Scripture:

"Keep me as the apple of your eye." Psalm 17:8.

"Your beauty should not come from outward adornment, such as braided hair and the wearing of gold jewelry and fine clothes. Instead, it should be that of your inner self, the unfading beauty of a gentle and quiet spirit, which is of great worth in God's sight." 1 Peter 3:3–4.

Her teaching echoed what Brian, as the voice of God, had spoken: inward beauty is the most important quality for a woman to have. She proclaimed the truth that we were each created in God's image and that we are beautiful in his eyes. She taught us how valuable we are to God and that he delights in us.

Next, Ann stepped again to the podium, where she introduced Catherine and Lydia, asking them to sing a song for us. Catherine has weathered many difficult seasons in her life, losing three children to a rare genetic condition, all within their first year of life. Such pain would cause many to lose faith or become bitter, but not Catherine. She is rock solid and full of the joy of the Lord.

As Catherine moved to the front, I recalled, four years earlier, her standing at the bedside of her daughter Ruthann just moments before she passed away. Family and friends were gathered around this tiny baby girl, praying and hoping for the miracle that never came. Tears streamed down our cheeks as Ruthann took her final breath and entered into God's presence. I will never forget what happened next. Through their tears and with heavy hearts, Catherine, her husband, Dierk, and her brother Bobby began worshiping our heavenly Father in song. No anger, no bitterness. Just faith. Yes, Catherine is rock solid in her faith and such an inspiration to many. I was so glad that she was part of Jeni's celebration.

The tape was cued up as Catherine and Lydia announced that they would sing "My Redeemer Lives." Many of us just closed our eyes as they sang, listening to the words, soaking up the sweet presence of the Lord that was in the room. Their love for Jesus was so evident as they sang. We were all deeply touched. When they finished, the room was very quiet. Ann then announced that it was time for us to share our letters and gifts with Jeni.

14

SHARING
WORDS
OF WISDOM

"MANY OF THE LADIES HERE TONIGHT have brought letters and gifts for you, Jeni," Ann said. "And there are others who could not attend but who sent theirs ahead of time. I will read those to you first."

At this point, Jeni moved her chair closer to the podium. I sat there with great expectation of what each woman would share with my daughter. Most in the room were seasoned women of God, and I was reminded of the scripture found in Titus 2:3–5 where it talks about the older women teaching the younger. I knew these letters would not only be enjoyable this night but also be a valuable source of guidance and encouragement for Jeni in the years to come.

Ann began by reading Grandma Molitor's letter to Jeni. Mom Molitor was there with us, but she had recently lost much of the use of her eyes to macular degeneration. Penned by my father-in-law, this is what her letter said:

Dear Granddaughter,

Finding a horseshoe is superstitiously thought to be a sign of good luck. Your Great Aunt Virginia gave this pin to me over forty years ago. You don't need such a symbol, as your "good luck" began on the day you were born to Brian and Kathy.

They felt such joy at having a daughter to join their two boys. Your mom has always enjoyed guiding you in every aspect of your maturity, and your dad is your greatest admirer; whenever you, your dad and I are together, he never fails to say, "Isn't she lovely!"

I was not as fortunate, as I grew up without a father, or brothers and sisters. Actually, most of the time without a mother, as she had to teach in various towns, while I lived with my grandmother in West Branch. That makes me especially aware of the loving and caring relationship that is obvious among all the members of your family. If you need to look for a role model or a heroine, look no further than your own special mother.

Grandpa and I watch with great pleasure your growing maturity, your sweet disposition and your abilities in sports. Add to all these ingredients your strong Christian environment and your path to a successful future is assured—a "slam dunk" as your generation might say.

Love to you,
Grandma Molitor

As Jeni walked over to her grandmother to receive a hug and the horseshoe-shaped pin, I quietly thanked the Lord for giving me such a wonderful mother-in-law. You see, none of the typical mother-in-law jokes have ever applied to me, as I have always cherished Brian's mom and consider our relationship to be a great blessing. I am also thankful for the beautiful role model she has been for Jeni and me. While losing one's eyesight would cause many to become angry, depressed or bitter, she has handled it with incredible grace. We have never once heard her complain, and she continues to be a great joy to those around her. Grandma Molitor is a true inspiration to her family.

Next, Ann opened another letter, this time from my own mother. Though her sight had not failed her, Mom has had difficulty getting around and uses a walker. Just a few days before the celebration, she had received the news that my dad's cancer had returned, so she had come with a heavy heart. For these reasons, we had asked Ann to read Mom's letter. This is what she had written:

Dear Jeni,

Thirteen years ago, your mother, with the help of the Lord, gave birth to a beautiful baby girl whose name is Jenifer. As your grandmother, I was very happy and proud to think that the Lord blessed me with a little granddaughter.

I have watched you grow up over the years with the guidance of your mom and dad. They have done a wonderful job.

Jeni, you are at a new threshold in your life of turning away from childish things and becoming a beautiful young lady.

May the Lord guide you in the coming years to the fulfillment of your dreams.

With much love,

Grandma Hayes

Tears filled my mother's eyes as she gazed at Jeni while Ann read the letter. My mom was unable to have more children after I was born, so to her, the sun rises and sets on our four children. When Ann finished, Jeni once again walked over to the table where both grandmothers were sitting and gave her Grandma Hayes a hug. One by one, the other women began to come to the podium to share with Jeni their letters and gifts that they had brought.

My friend Carla came to the front and pulled up a chair facing Jeni so that she could speak to her eye-to-eye, woman-to-woman. Carla and I have gone through the births, deaths, and weddings of our loved ones together. I recalled countless times over many years when we had cried together, laughed together, and—of course—ate chocolate together. It was great to have her at Jeni's rite-of-passage ceremony. Here are some excerpts from Carla's letter:

Dear Jeni,

When I think of you, I think of constancy. You have somehow managed to maintain a sweetness of spirit and a gentleness of heart from the time you were a little girl until now.... My gift of a Concordance to you reflects the most important step of growth for me as a believer. Years ago, a Concordance opened a whole new world for me. I discovered the thrill of discovering new truths and of finding old truths in a new way. Suddenly, studying the Bible became my greatest desire and something I looked forward to every day....

I have tears in my eyes as I write this. It is such an honor to sow seed into your life. Though it seems our paths have gone separate ways these past few years, they truly run parallel. I have kept my eye on you from a distance and I'm so blessed by what I see. Stay pure of heart, Jeni. There is a wonderful, fulfilling life waiting for you.

Now, here are excerpts from some of the other letters that evening:

Look at you now—all grown up and beautiful inside and out! That's so important to remember as you're growing up. Being a female in today's society makes it so difficult to have a good self-esteem, not only in our looks, but in our bodies. We see on the TV and in the magazines how perfect and beautiful the women are. I struggled with that not as bad in high school, but in college. I was so focused on my outward appearance and I wanted to be popular and to fit in with the beautiful people. I tried to be one of them and I was miserable trying...Please remember as you enter high school and college, how important it is to keep your heart pure.

What I want to impress on your thinking tonight is that YOU are a one-of-a-kind creation by Almighty God, infinitely valuable because there never has been and never will be anyone else like you! that God will reveal to you how wonderfully valuable you are to Him!

The one life lesson I would offer you is summed up in the words, "Don't settle!" Don't settle for what the world would offer. Instead, hold out for God's best for you. The Lord has a wonderful plan for your life, and if you live a life of no compromise, you will emerge as a woman of Godly character and wisdom.

Be true to the name God gave you through your parents: Jenifer means "White Wave." The symbolic meaning is Pure and Yielding. Elizabeth means Consecrated to God. Decision-making will become more frequent for you now and the consequences of your decisions will begin to hold greater impact as time goes on.

You have been created with purpose and a future filled with hope. I thank God for you and your willingness to place your life in God's hands. A few words that I might speak to you from my life experience would be: Whatever you feed is what will prosper. If you feed the flesh, it will prosper, and if you feed the spirit, it will prosper. I believe you will feed your spirit and that you will become more and more mature in your discernment of the truth, "evolving" into a fruitful woman of God who will fulfill her purpose.

Even though we are from different countries and different cultures, there are things that are common in the world.

Don't be afraid to live for Christ and to hold your integrity high. People will respect you for it even though they may not voice it.

Set boundaries for yourself. For when you are at your weakest, these boundaries the Lord will bring to your remembrance and He will give you the strength to overcome. Remember, your body is the temple of the Holy Spirit and anyone who loves you will respect you and not try to force you or put you on a guilt trip to prove anything that is against what the Bible says.

Be very careful of self-condemnation. It is a tool the enemy uses to keep us trapped or bound. Jesus has set you free, for who the Son sets free is free indeed. He will never let you down!

Keeping your eyes fixed on Him assures you of His Love, His protection and His incredible plan for your life. Taking your eyes off of Him causes you to doubt your worth, compare yourself to others and fall into the world's trap of superficial happiness. Only He know the plans He has for you, plans to prosper you and not to harm you, to give you a future and a hope. Jeremiah 29:11.

God wants to show you that He is in control and willing to gracefully guide you in the craziness of your life. You need to always give Him the chance to do that! And when things in your life seem out of control, talk to the One who took the time to fold His own burial cloth. John 20:6–7.

Becoming a woman of God begins now. As you enter high school, your actions and attitude will always be on display to others as well as to God. If we live each day seeking His guidance and treasuring Him in our hearts, then we can live out being the Worthy Woman.

How exciting it is to know that you gave your heart and life to Christ at an early age! You've grown up in a home where you've been taught by example to value Godly attributes and characteristics, to become a strong, but gentle and sensitive, responsible and loving young lady. Now I bless you and pray for you as you continue to strive for excellence and a deeper intimacy with the Lord, an intimacy that will bring many opportunities into each new day. I pray those opportunities will birth great blessings and victories in the years ahead of you. On this special day, I honor, esteem and affirm you as a young woman and as a daughter of the King!

Love God. Sometimes we try to complicate Christianity, when in reality all we must do is love Him. If we love Him, we will live for Him. If we love Him, we will love others. If we love Him, we will make it through every trial that we may face.

When the last letter was read, I stood and walked over to Jeni, struggling to contain my emotions. So many things flooded my thoughts and my heart: my intense love for her and my deep gratitude for each woman who had poured out her encouragement to our daughter.

It was time for me to read my letter to Jeni, and through the tears, this is what I read:

To my loving daughter Jeni,

Where do I begin? I sit here at the computer, weeping. My heart is so full of love for you. As I've told you so many times, you will only fully understand just how much "Daddy" and I love you when you become a parent yourself someday.

From the moment I saw you (and even while in my womb) I have loved you. You have been a joy beyond description. I treasure so many memories of times spent when you were first a baby and then a small child. The closeness that we shared is a precious thought to me. I remember how, as an infant, you would look up at me as I would feed you, and begin to smile as our eyes lovingly locked. Eventually, you grew to love playing house. I loved those times too—playing make-believe with all the plastic foods and dishes. And then there was the Playmobil house with all the little people. I was sad when you got too old and no longer wanted to play with them anymore. Finally, one day, I packed them up and put them in the attic, and I knew then that you were beginning to grow up too fast for me.

The years seem to go so fast. There were piano & ballet lessons, karate, skating and swimming lessons, too. There were practices for plays at church and worship dance. A train trip to Chicago when you turned ten, and then another trip to Florida together to visit Mr. & Mrs. Bennett. What fun times we've had together! Then came basketball, volleyball, track and cheerleading. How blessed your dad & I have been to watch you excel, grow & mature. How wonderful to see all the gifts and talents your Father in heaven has equipped you with. Your beautiful voice amazes me, and your ability and passion to nurture others is a wonderful blessing. More than all these things though Jen, the things that touch my heart the most is the way you show love to those around you and the sweet spirit you have always had. You are one of the most kind, thoughtful & loving people I have ever known. I can't express how grateful I am to call you "daughter." Your deep concern for others, your unselfish ways have ministered to your family and others many, many times. You have blessed me so many times by loving me and accepting me when I was unlovable. Thank you, sweetheart, for all the encouraging words, the little notes you've left me and for all the hugs and pats on the arm or back.

I treasure our friendship more than you can imagine and I look forward to a lifetime of closeness as we pursue, together, all that God has for both of us. I recommit myself to you, tonight, to help you become that mighty woman of God that He has called you to be in the kingdom—for such a time as this.

I love you very, very much,
Mom

┌─────────┐
│ **15** │
└─────────┘

GIFTS
ARE
GIVEN

 JUST AS EACH LETTER SPOKE VOLUMES TO JENIFER, so did the gifts that she received. The offerings to this young woman-in-the-making were powerful symbols of what was happening within Jenifer during that evening. Some of the gifts were symbolic, some sentimental, and others very practical.

After I finished reading my letter to Jeni, I presented her with my gift, a gold chain necklace, upon which hung a cross. I hope that as the years go by, it will be a gentle reminder of her special night but, more important, it will be a symbol of how much her mother loves her.

Wanda, a dear family friend we've known for several years, sent Jeni a pin, in the shape of a key, that had the name of Jesus engraved on it. Her note to Jeni read: "The little key speaks of how the fear of the Lord is the key to life and happiness."

Hope, who had written to Jeni about Jesus' burial cloth, gave Jeni a large piece of cloth, carefully folded inside a basket. She explained that she wanted it to be something Jeni could use to remember that God loves her and as long as she continues to stay close to Him, He will take care of her.

Marguerite, Heidi's sister, gave Jeni a beautiful glass treasure box that had Jeni's monogram "J.E.M." and Proverbs 31:25–26 engraved on the lid. Marguerite challenged Jeni to remember that the best treasure in this life is your relationship to God.

Jeni received many great gifts, such as the *Strong's Concordance*, a beautiful heart-shaped watch, and writing journals. She also received a couple of books to meditate on, one entitled *Daughters* and the other entitled *Book of Joy*. Still, another woman had actually taken the time to make a collage for Jeni that had pictures and phrases depicting a young woman who would walk in righteousness.

Our former office manager, Marge, brought Jeni a blue-beaded butterfly bracelet and matching necklace. In a portion of her letter, she explained the meaning of her gift in this way: Just as a butterfly develops and is transformed by the God of all creation into a thing of beauty, you are also now emerging into young adulthood.

Ann presented Jeni with a beautiful white and yellow gold necklace pendant that had two dolphins forming a heart. It was to remind Jeni of our trip to Florida some years earlier. Ann recalled how Jeni, even when she was very young, had an understanding of truth—that God created the dolphin and that she knew that we all have a Creator and "that through him all things were made; without him nothing was made that has been made" (John 1:3).

My trusted friend Karen gave Jenifer a plaque that read "A girl is all God has with which to make a woman." She explained that Jeni was born with all she needs to become a woman and that her upbringing has preserved that. She reminded Jeni that because she accepted the Lord at an early age, growing into a woman is even easier.

My mom surprised Jeni with a unique gift: my first pair of white walking shoes from when I was a baby. She had encouraged Jeni to walk in righteousness all the days of her life.

Each gift, so carefully chosen and given with such thoughtfulness, strengthened and encouraged Jeni that she was accepted by the older women. Once the letters were read and the gifts given, we were nearing the end of this part of the celebration. However, there was one last letter to be read—and perhaps it was the most important letter of all. Brian now entered the room, after patiently waiting for over three hours in the hotel lobby. I'll let him tell you about what happened next...

16

A FATHER'S
BLESSING

 *Brian here...*

AS JENI'S CELEBRATION WENT ON, I sat in the lobby waiting for my cell phone to ring. That would be the signal that it was time for me to join Kathy and the others to pray a blessing over Jenifer. We were convinced that a child of either gender needs the affirmation of a father or father figure to secure his or her identity. For this reason, I was to be present during the time of prayer to identity as a woman.

As I sat there, and then paced, and then sat again, I wondered what my daughter was going through. Had Kathy read her my letter yet? Since I would not be in the room at the time the letters would be read, I had asked her to read it in my place. I hoped that its intended meaning would come through as Kathy read it. Nervous dad. As I waited, I recalled how powerful each of Jeni's brother's rites of passage was and prayed that God would touch Jeni in much the same way. I need not have worried.

When, after three hours, the phone finally rang, I literally jumped up, fumbled with the phone, and promptly dropped it on the hard tile of the lobby. Nervous dad. Anyway, the phone survived long enough for me to hear Kathy's voice inviting me to come to the room to pray over Jeni. Hanging up, I then... [you pick]

    A. walked calmly down the hall toward the celebration.

    B. sprinted, nearly flooring a startled hotel guest on the
       way to his room.

If you picked A, you don't yet have a daughter. It was B.

    Arriving at the door, I knocked, and my wife led me into the room. I could feel the presence of the Lord as I entered. There, sitting in a chair in the middle of the room, was my beautiful daughter, waiting for us to pray a blessing over her. I made my way to her trying to think of what to pray. So many thoughts were surging through my mind. Just as I reached Jeni, I heard Kathy's voice. For a second I thought she said that she had *forgotten to read my letter to Jeni.* Then I heard her repeat it, and I knew I was in trouble. Kathy said that since I was now there, I "might as well read it to her myself." Oh boy...

    Trying to compose myself, I quietly took the letter, sat down facing Jenifer, and slowly read my letter to her. I will share parts of it with you.

Dear Jeni,

    Or should I say "Peaches" or "Lambie"? My precious daughter, it is my great joy to write this letter to share just a tiny bit of how much I love you.

    It is hard to believe that you are a young woman now. I can remember the day that you were born. In fact, I can remember the instant that you came into this world and the joy that I felt to know that God had given me a daughter! On that day, I noticed how beautiful and gentle you were. Those wonderful qualities continue to this day.

    It has really been fun to watch you grow over the past thirteen years. You continue to be beautiful and gentle, but along with that you have acquired a tremendous sense of humor, insight beyond your years, and a deep concern for others. I can honestly say that you have never disappointed me in any way, and I marvel at the incredible qualities that God has placed within you. You are truly the apple of my eye!

I am your greatest earthly fan, advocate, protector, and cheerleader. While there is breath in my body, this will never change. I am looking forward to watching you grow, mature, play, and eventually raise a family of your own. I am thrilled to know that you also have another fan, advocate, protector, and cheerleader. This one has no limitations and will watch over you for an eternity. He is your heavenly Father, and all his ways are perfect. Honey, stay close to God in all you do and watch his plan unfold for your wonderful life.

Jeni, you are the joy of my life, and I truly delight in you just exactly as you are! I wouldn't trade you for anyone in the world, and I am so proud that you are my daughter.

Blessings and more love than you can imagine!

Your father,

Brian D. Molitor

After I finished reading, it was time to pray a blessing on the beautiful young woman. Kathy and I stood in front of Jeni and laid our hands upon her head. The first words out of my mouth followed the same pattern that her brothers heard during their times of blessing.

"Jeni, you are my beloved daughter, in whom I am well pleased."

After that, Kathy and many of the other women prayed blessings over Jeni, speaking life-giving words into her spirit. Together, we affirmed her womanhood, her identity, her destiny, and her many gifts, talents, and abilities. It was a truly powerful time. After a few minutes, I backed away and watched as the older women blessed the younger, just as God intended it to happen from the beginning.

When the prayers and blessings ended, a young woman stood up from the chair that had been occupied by a girl only minutes before. Tall, beaming with confidence, Jeni faced the group and thanked them with a smile. The tears and hugs continued to flow for quite a while afterward.

Finally, after basking in the Lord's presence for a time, we sensed that everything had been accomplished that he had wanted done. By then, it was late, but no one seemed to care. When you are in the company of the King, time seems suspended, and such was the case that night. We had been touched by his presence, and more important, so had Jeni.

Kathy and I took a moment to thank all the women who had come, but words could not express our deep gratitude. It was so much more than we could have ever imagined.

Soon, it was time to pack up Jeni's gifts, letters, and memories and walk out into the night. That evening I had the honor of driving two women home. I have never been prouder.

PART 5

🍃

CREATING A PLAN FOR YOUR DAUGHTER

17

FOUNDATIONS FOR YOUR DAUGHTER'S CELEBRATION

OVER THE YEARS, Kathy and I have had the honor of hosting, attending, and assisting with the design of countless rites of passage. Based upon those experiences, we compiled the following answers to the most common questions about celebrations. We offer them to assist you when planning an event for your own daughter.

IS A RITE OF PASSAGE OPTIONAL?

We believe that a properly planned celebration is an essential part of every young person's life. To put this in the plainest terms possible, a rite of passage is not an option; it is a necessity. There is no alternative to acknowledging a girl's transition into womanhood if we truly want her to succeed. A big birthday party will not do it. A trip to Disney World will not do it. A transitional event is a must.

HOW DO I PREPARE MY DAUGHTER?

As part of the ongoing, lifelong mentoring discussions with your daughter, it is good to explain the scope and intent of the event to her when she is quite young. However, many parents will find themselves in the same situation that we were in with our oldest son. They will not have years to prepare their child for the transitional event and will simply have to start wherever they are in the process.

For those parents who have the time, it's best to hold extensive discussions with your child prior to the celebration. Your talks should focus on the rite of passage itself and what it means for the young woman's future. Clearly, these discussions set up vital aspects of the event itself, even though they may take place months or years beforehand. Fathers and mothers should be mentoring their daughters all along, but especially in the months prior to their rites of passage. It will be good to talk through new expectations, changing roles, and any new responsibilities that will be given to your daughter after the event takes place.

WHAT IS THE BEST AGE FOR A GIRL'S RITE OF PASSAGE?

No two children are exactly alike, and no two children mature at exactly the same age. Therefore, one child may be ready to accept new levels of responsibility at age thirteen while a sibling may take longer to mature, so do not feel as if you are locked into a certain age for the celebration.

In addition to maturity level, other factors influence when you should host your celebration. For example, if your family is going through a particularly hectic time (such as a change in location or a serious illness of a loved one) near your daughter's birthday, you should consider delaying the celebration for a month or two. I would not recommend hosting a rite of passage for a child younger than thirteen years of age.

Each parent or mentor should prayerfully consider whether the child is ready for this life-changing event. It is clearly more art than science, so I cannot give you any exact guidelines to follow for scheduling a rite of passage. Some girls will be ready for the added responsibility and freedom much earlier than others. Others will take more time to reach the level of maturity and understanding required for the celebration to be truly meaningful. I will offer this one piece of advice, though. If you are in doubt about a young person's ability to comprehend the celebration's meaning, wait a few months, do some additional teaching on the subject of womanhood and maturity, and then schedule the event.

Having said all of that, I believe that there is something very special about affirming adulthood during the early teen years. Many cultures throughout history have identified the teen years as the time when their children make the transition into adulthood. In our modern culture, we clearly recognize that the teen years are unique, but unfortunately, we have not known what to do with them! Rather than fearing this period and viewing it as a time of impending rebellion, we can now begin to celebrate it as a time of orderly transition.

WHAT ABOUT MY OLDER DAUGHTER?

What about those parents who have an older daughter who has never had a rite of passage? Have these young women missed out on the opportunity to grow into mature adulthood? Not at all! This type of celebration is extremely effective for a young person of nineteen, twenty-one, or even older. Indeed, this ceremony can be a life-changing event even for people who have reached their twenties and thirties. The old adage "better late than never" certainly applies here. When creating an event for an older child, the celebration can simply become an affirmation of the transition that has taken place rather than the actual event at which the transformation into adulthood occurs. We have helped create rites of passage for young adults that truly changed their lives. No matter what the age, each of us needs the affirmation and confirmation that we are received as adults by the broader community or by the adult members of our family.

While this type of ceremony can be connected to a young person's actual birthday, it may also be linked with other special events occurring later in life, such as graduating from high school or entering college. In other words, you do not have to wait until a particular birthday rolls around to host the celebration. Use any opportunity you have, as soon as you sense that the time is right. You and your child will be glad you did. Our entire society will benefit as well.

WHAT IS MOM'S ROLE? WHAT IS DAD'S ROLE?

Another central issue concerns the role of a girl's mother and father in her celebration. Kathy and I agree that whenever possible, the mom should plan the ceremony and serve as the hostess. Dad may want to spend some special time with his daughter before the gathering. He may do such things as take her to lunch or dinner before the evening's celebration. In addition, he may want to write her a keepsake letter that she can open when she returns home, or that Mom can read aloud during the rite-of-passage event. The bottom line is this: we have concluded that it is better if the father not host or attend the main portion of his daughter's celebration. That is Mom's job.

I realize this is a very emotional subject that takes some time to think through. Nevertheless, a celebration marking a girl's transition to womanhood is best accomplished in the presence of other women. However, I feel just as strongly that a father or father figure must be present to bless the daughter at the conclusion of the ceremony. So much of a child's identity is drawn from her father's blessing (or lack thereof), so this is key. Moms can help dads understand and enjoy all that takes place there by videotaping the proceedings and by taking some photos as well. It is an emotional time for everyone involved, so some extra concern, communication, and caring will help the rite of passage be a smooth and rewarding event for the whole family.

In a situation where there is no mother to participate, a single dad will need to locate an appropriate woman to help with his daughter's rite of passage. A family member or someone from the women's ministry at a local church will make an excellent stand-in for a mom who is unable to participate.

DOES THE RITE OF PASSAGE HAVE TO BE A "SPIRITUAL" EVENT?

I am not aware of any culture, past or present, that held rites of passage for its youth and yet failed to embrace the deeply spiritual aspects of the ceremony. While these cultures would never agree on one approach to theology, they all clearly agree on one foundational truth—life is more than what is seen with our natural eyes. In sad contrast, our own society, in all of its arrogance and ignorance about God's sustaining grace, tries to pull farther and farther away from its deeply rooted spirituality. What a sad mistake.

We must not allow our children's rites of passage to become fancy birthday parties devoid of spirituality, God, or religious foundations. To do so would be a grave mistake. However, please understand that parents do not have to be spiritual superstars for the celebration to be genuine. They simply need to have a real desire to know God and follow him to the best of their abilities. This sincerity, not perfect attendance at church or deacon board membership, will be seen, admired, and emulated by their daughters.

HOW WILL PRAYER PLAY A PART?

If there is ever a season to set aside distractions and spend time in reflective prayer for your daughter, it is prior to her celebration. There is no substitute! The impact of prayer will be evident in many ways during the celebration. Parents should prayerfully consider whom to invite, where to have the gathering, and what to include on the agenda for their daughter's rite of passage. These are all-important aspects of the event, and nothing should be taken for granted. Prayer will help the women know what to write, say, and give to your young woman-in-the-making. Prayer will seal the blessing for your daughter when the celebration ends. Prayer is the greatest assurance you can have that your celebration will accomplish its immediate and eternal goals.

IS BIGGER REALLY BETTER?

In a word...no. Our society continually preaches that big is better than small, fancy is better than plain, and enough money will assure success in any endeavor. Do not get caught up in any of this nonsense when it comes to your daughter's celebration. A prayerfully planned celebration held in a cement-block basement and attended by just a few women will be infinitely more powerful than some godless, grand production in a fancy conference center. Quality, not quantity, is key here. Keep praying about your event, and the answers to when, where, and who should attend will soon be evident.

HOW DO I MANAGE THE EVENT ITSELF?
WHERE DO I START?

Naturally, there are many options, and you should feel free to be creative. However, here are some general suggestions that can help with the planning process. It is a great idea to get others involved, just as we did.

Choose a Practical Location

Remember that the celebration is primarily designed to allow a young woman to receive blessings, affirmations, and encouragement from older women. Thus, the event may be as simple or as elaborate as you choose. The impact will come from the depth of what is shared rather than from the setting itself. Therefore, many different locations can be appropriate, including a home, hotel, church, campsite, or rented meeting hall. Just be sure to select a location that will comfortably hold the number of people you invite and allow sufficient room for all of your planned activities.

Timing

Just as there are many alternatives for where to hold a celebration, there are many options for when one can be scheduled. You can plan yours for any day of the week, but you need to consider work schedules, school obligations, possible travel time for out-of-town guests, and other potential conflicts. Most celebrations that we have attended have been held on weekends. Be sure to allow sufficient time so that you are not rushed. We have never attended a celebration that took less than three hours, so plan accordingly. This once-in-a-lifetime event must not be rushed or overshadowed by any other conflicting event.

Arrange for Refreshments

It is a nice touch when some refreshments are provided during the celebration. They may be eaten before or after the event. Options include a formal dinner, snacks, a cake, beverages, or any other combination that is appropriate for your girl's special event. However, please do not think that you must have a catered dinner to make the celebration a success. In fact, food and refreshments are add-ons to the celebration. They are not essentials. My personal preference is to have light snacks before the celebration. This allows time for stragglers to arrive. I avoid a full dinner, because it takes a great deal of time that is better spent on the celebration itself.

Contacting and Preparing the Guests

The number of women attending the celebration may range from three to thirty. I would discourage a gathering larger than that, as it creates problems with space and overextends the length of the event. Here again, more is not necessarily better. Your daughter will be blessed that just a few women cared enough to attend her special event. She will also know if some came simply out of obligation. You would not want any of your female guests sitting there preoccupied with other things, so choose wisely.

Invitations should be sent out *at least* two weeks before the event. However, four weeks notice, or more, is preferable in order to allow time for the adjustment of busy schedules. You can use our letter in this book as a model or simply write your own. Just be sure to include place, time, and all other details, including what you are requesting the women to do at the event. Don't assume that they will initially understand the rite-of-passage concept. Lovingly explain what you are doing, give the reasons for the event, and state specifically what you need from them. Have them contact you before the celebration if they have any questions so that they come prepared to properly minister to your daughter.

Skits and Dramas

Skits and dramas can be powerful tools for teaching life lessons to your daughter at the celebration. They take the old adage of "a picture is worth a thousand words" to a new dimension—a *demonstration* is worth a thousand pictures! Of course, this means that whatever skits you choose must be designed to lovingly and powerfully teach lessons that your daughter will need for the future. Let me head off some potential skit problems with a few dos and don'ts:

DO be very creative in your skit design. There is no shortage of challenges that we face in life, so there are countless life lessons that can be powerfully portrayed in a skit or drama. Today's woman must deal with self-esteem, friendship, work, education, choices, purity, faith, and a wide variety of other issues. Any of these are great foundations for skits. They do not have to be funny or elaborate to be effective. Just make sure they are appropriate to your daughter's age, maturity level, and life experiences.

DO select your participants wisely. Make sure that each person involved in a skit is credible and able to handle the tasks assigned. By this, I mean do not have a relative who is an avowed atheist attempt to portray a message about the importance of a spiritual foundation for life! This will not be well received. Also, be sure you do not assign someone to be part of a skit if she tends to want to attract attention to herself. Putting a would-be comedienne in front of a dozen other people is a recipe for disaster in the context of a celebration. The focus must be on the lesson, not on the people taking part in the skit. Select participants who are levelheaded, outgoing, and not prone to act silly. Then make sure they have time to prepare for their parts.

DO NOT make the skit your ultimate "weapon." A skit is not the appropriate vehicle for "finally" getting a particular point across to your daughter. It is not to be used as a weapon to browbeat a young woman about sins of the past. A frustrated parent may have been talking with the daughter for years about the need for better grooming, industriousness, spirituality, or any other subject. The night of her special celebration is not the time to ram the point home one more time. This would be a lecture in disguise. Please do not bother. It would cheapen the rest of the event and probably ensure another few years of noncompliance by your daughter. I encourage you to trust the celebration process and allow your child to grow toward maturity after it is over.

DO NOT design a skit that would embarrass your daughter. Avoid humiliating your daughter by pointing out her weaknesses or her past failures. For example, if she has been in trouble with authority in school, a skit about respecting teachers would be a bad idea. Also, if she has struggled with drugs or alcohol, a skit about the dangers of substance abuse would be inappropriate. The young woman would perceive this as an attempt to embarrass her in front of respected elders. Clearly, that is not your goal.

Here is a final hint: When you design your skits, be sure that *all the props will be available when you need them.* You do not want to be making changes at the last second because a prop is unavailable, broken, or just overlooked.

Be Open to Including Alternative Activities

For various reasons, some people will not feel comfortable designing skits or dramas for their daughter's celebration. Either they are unsure of their abilities to create a skit, or they determine that their daughter will not favorably respond to a skit. In these instances, there are alternatives that can make the celebration interesting, powerful, and memorable for your young woman or daughter.

One alternative is to prepare a poster board or sheet of paper with your daughter's name at the top. Pass the board around to the attendees and have them write two words that describe your daughter. Words like *diligent, strong, kind, smart,* and *loving* will greatly encourage her and help her see herself as others do.

Another alternative is for the mom or grandmother to share positive stories and remembrances about the girl from her childhood. These must be positive and not embarrassing for the young woman. Her first significant accomplishment, first act of kindness, or other such notable event will remind your daughter that she has had a positive impact on her family and her world since she first arrived.

Yet another alternative or addition to skits and dramas is to present your daughter with a scrapbook of her photos and accomplishments from the past. This type of presentation would make an excellent foundation for the young woman's future.

The bottom line is this: The celebration should be designed in a way that creates powerful, positive memories for your daughter. She will remember the sights, sounds, messages, people, and emotions for a lifetime. Take time to design the celebration with this in mind.

As a final thought, remember that the underlying motive for the celebration is love. Thankfully, love covers a multitude of sins, errors, and mistakes, so you do not need to worry if something does not go quite as planned. Love will take care of it. As you plan your celebration, please just relax and follow your heart. It is going to be great!

A VISION FOR YOUR CHILDREN'S CHILDREN

Our vision is for these celebrations to become part of the Molitor family culture for generations to come. Once we held our initial celebration for our oldest son, Christopher, we had three years to prepare for Steven's celebration, five years to prepare for Jenifer's, and seven years to prepare for Daniel's. We used that time to have ongoing discussions (mentoring) about adulthood, maturity, and growing responsibility with each of our children. We also used that time to bless our children with words, touch, and prayer. As a result, each of them eagerly anticipated his or her impending day of transition. The concept of rites of passage is now becoming ingrained into the very fabric of both our immediate and extended family—so much so that we look forward to participating in the celebrations of our children's children. The point here is that you should introduce the celebration concept to your children as soon as you possibly can. If you missed this opportunity with your first child, do not miss it for your second child. If you missed it for all of your children, do not miss it for your grandchildren. Many lives will be changed as a result!

18

NEW HOPE
FOR A TROUBLED
DAUGHTER

THIS CHAPTER IS ALL ABOUT RESTORATION and reconciliation of our troubled girls to their parents and to their Creator. This is achievable; however, first we need to understand the type of girl we are talking about. Then we will consider (1) how to look past her rebellion to see something very positive and (2) how to pay attention to what is happening in the rest of the family. Finally, we will look at some practical ways to keep hope alive in families struggling with their own prodigal daughters.

WAYWARD DAUGHTERS

I am often asked whether parents should implement a plan of mentoring, blessing, and rites of passage for a daughter who is currently rebellious or involved with drugs, alcohol, sex, and other negative behaviors. My response is unquestionably *yes!* However, some modifications need to be made in order for the whole process to work. A plan of gentle mentoring and careful, intentional blessing, capped off with a customized rite of passage, will help get many of our troubled or wayward girls back on the right path.

The term *wayward* is an old-fashioned one, but it still accurately describes many young females today. According to Webster's, *wayward* means "insistent on having one's own way, contrary to others' advice, wishes, or commands; headstrong, disobedient. Conforming to no fixed rule, or pattern; unpredictable."

All too often, young women today insist on going their own way despite the advice of those in authority. Many of the troubled youth are latchkey kids who grew up without parental supervision. Others have had fathers or mothers abandon them, leaving no positive role model to follow. Certainly, divorce has been a major cause of hurt and anger for many youth today, both male and female. Perhaps it is easy to see why these conditions foster rebellion in young people. However, there are also many troubled, disobedient, and unpredictable teenagers who were raised in "good" homes with parents who loved them to the best of their ability. In these instances, we all search for answers to the often unspoken question, What went wrong?

WHAT WENT WRONG?

Our children are bombarded each day with conflicting messages about life, adulthood, sexuality, morality, and other issues. Raging hormones and bouncing brain chemistry create massive mood swings in even the most stable teenagers. Lost love and broken hearts cause many teens to do things that they will regret years later. Peer pressure pumps our daughters full of ideas that seem right in the short term but yield long-term negative consequences. Once reserved for their male counterparts, now drug- and alcohol-related problems, road rage, sexually transmitted diseases, and even nights in jail all have become reality for today's young women. Parents of children caught in any of these traps are hit by the inevitable fallout of guilt, frustration, shame, fear, embarrassment, and legal woes that accompany the wayward behavior.

As parents, Kathy and I realize that we have made many mistakes in raising our children. Things we *should* have said, we did not. Things we *should not* have said, we did. We could have spent more time with each child; we should have been stricter in some areas and more lenient in others; we should have…you get the message here. Of course, we all could have done better raising our children. However, none of us was, is, or will be perfect. This is why our daughters still need a heavenly Father, so that he can make up for our shortcomings.

THE POWER OF APOLOGY

Our failings provide wonderful opportunities for the powerful concepts of repentance and forgiveness to do their marvelous work. Many times, we have had to go to our children and ask for their forgiveness because of something that was said or done. It is amazing how quickly this simple act reconnects hearts and frees our souls. Parents, especially fathers, must realize that apologizing to their children when they fail them is not a sign of weakness but rather a sign of strength. Despite this fact, some fathers and mothers struggle to ask for forgiveness or to admit that they have ever done anything wrong. We must realize that an apology is likely the best place to start rebuilding the foundations of trust when we have fallen short as parents. Sometimes, our daughter's waywardness has been caused by something that we have done. In other words, we may hold the keys to the chains that keep her bound.

WHEN A FATHER'S HEART TURNS, SO WILL THE CHILD'S

It is important to realize that the simple act of apologizing to and asking for forgiveness from a child is far more than a "religious" act. It opens the door for God's miraculous intervention. Not long ago, I got a phone call from Peter (not his real name), a man who had attended one of our Malachi Global Foundation men's retreats. Through tears, Peter explained that he had reluctantly agreed to attend the retreat at the urging of some friends. While there, I had taught about the power of a father's touch and that, at times, we use our hands to harm instead of to heal our children. Peter explained that when I spoke about the power to harm or heal, he felt as if lightning hit him, right in the midst of hundreds of other men. He was immediately taken back to a time when a "friend" had counseled him and his wife on how to discipline their two daughters.

The advice was to never allow the girls to give the parents any back talk and, at the first sign of any challenge to the parents' authority, to severely "discipline" the children. His method of choice? He instructed Peter to slap their faces—hard. As young parents wanting to raise their children correctly, Peter and his wife followed the misguided mentor's advice, and whenever their young daughters stepped out of line, Peter slapped them. In private, in public, wherever.

During our phone call, Peter explained that while he had stayed for the remainder of the men's retreat, he never heard another word that I said. He was consumed with grief at the emotional harm done to his precious daughters, now ages fourteen and seventeen. Naturally, by this point in the conversation, we both were weeping. I could hear the pain in his voice as the broken father continued.

Peter explained that following the retreat, he had driven home and literally run to his wife to explain what he had realized. Peter also did something that he had never done before during their eighteen years of marriage. He apologized to his wife for all that he had done wrong. This was followed by another first, as Peter began to weep in front of his wife for the first time ever. His heart had been wonderfully broken and then turned to his family. Soon, he and his wife began to cry together, and God brought healing into a strained relationship. Peter then called his daughters into the room, one at a time, and apologized for having ever slapped them in the face. In less than an hour after this remorseful father came home, all four of them melted together, crying, repenting, forgiving, and opening their hearts to one another.

Now, if the story ended there, it would be good enough. However, Peter added one more twist that showed the amazing power of a father's repentance as spoken of in Malachi 4:6. He explained that unbeknownst to anyone outside of his family, they had all been going through extensive counseling during the previous year. His home had been a living hell, a battleground with rage, yelling, swearing, throwing items, and slamming doors. Love had not dwelt in his house for years. It seems that after that amazing night when the heart of a father turned back to his family, things began to change, so much so that after just four weeks, Peter packed up his wife and daughters for their weekly trip to the counselor's office for their scheduled appointment. This time, instead of the family having individual sessions, Peter asked that they all be allowed to speak with the head counselor as a group. During that meeting, Peter explained what had happened and told of his family's desire to end the ongoing counseling. His rationale? They no longer needed it. The reaction of the counselor was predictable. She was horrified at the notion that such a dysfunctional group could make it on their own. Her initial predictions were that Peter's family would soon explode into a chaotic mess. Despite her objections, the family maintained that something profound had changed. During our conversation, Peter explained to me that the counselor then took the next two hours to interview each family member individually. She was trying to find a reason for them to continue with their long-term program of counseling. After the evening's sessions ended, this professional counselor came to an amazing conclusion. Something had changed. Healing that had eluded the family for years had somehow made its way into four hearts, and they no longer needed professional help. She released Peter and his family with a smile. They were healed, by the power of forgiveness and the miraculous turning of a father's heart to his wife and daughters.

THE NEED FOR A POSITIVE PATTERN

I am convinced that we fathers can help our daughters avoid the pitfalls of youth. A key to this is found in the final line of Webster's definition of *waywardness*, which reads, *"conforming to no fixed rule or pattern."*

In our society, there is no shortage of rules and patterns intended to control the day-to-day behavior of our youth. Parents establish rules for when to go to sleep, timetables for when the child needs to come home in the evenings, and specific instructions on how chores are to be done. Schools have rules about running in hallways, chewing gum, where to sit, and even when to go to the bathroom. Student athletes receive extensive coaching and instruction about particular plays or patterns in their respective sports.

No reasonable person would challenge the notion that these kinds of rules, patterns, and coaching are necessary for young people to learn basic expectations, standards, and boundaries. However, in contrast, few of our young females receive any coaching, patterns, or guidance about their impending womanhood. Most simply receive a few cryptic sound bites tossed at them at random intervals. Statements such as "It is time you grow up" or "Stop acting like a child" may mean something significant to the adult saying them, but to a young person they are open to a huge variance of interpretation. Statements like these are certainly not foundations upon which a young woman can build her future, and yet, they are often the only ones that she hears.

This is true even in "good" homes where the absence of a clear path to mature adulthood will encourage young females to try to blaze their own. Sadly, their pioneering often causes them to go in an unhealthy direction that results in waywardness, broken relationships, and damaged lives. Yet, even the most difficult cases can be turned around. Before we look any deeper into the subject of waywardness, I need to share an important thought with parents who may have a troubled daughter.

FREE WILL — FREE CHOICE

Some parents carry unnecessary guilt, blaming themselves for any and all problems experienced by their children. Those whose daughters have wandered away or gotten into trouble should consider the very real possibility that they did nothing seriously wrong in their upbringing. Remember, young people have free will and therefore make choices in life, just as we do. If they make good choices, they generally have a good life. Often, their own bad choices set the stage for some real problems in life. There is certainly biblical precedent for this.

Consider the account of creation in which our heavenly Father designs a wonderful world for his first children, Adam and Eve, to live in. These "children" had it made, right? Perfect weather, daily walks with God, no telemarketers, and a marriage made in heaven... All this, and yet, they blew it! With just a couple of bites, their bad choice put an end to paradise and opened their lives to pain, toil, death, and a host of other evils. Amazingly, Adam and Eve stepped smack in the middle of the *only* mess available on earth at the time. (Now, does that sound like any teenager that you know?) Despite the fact that their Father had done nothing wrong, these young folks were about to suffer the consequences of their own bad choice. The bottom line is this: do not allow guilt or condemnation to paralyze you because of how your children are doing at this moment. Whether your daughter is in trouble, in rebellion, or in prison, there is still hope as long as you stay engaged in the process. As long as the child is still alive, you can influence her with your renewed commitment to love her, pray for her, and bless her. Just as our heavenly Father did with his first children, we can cover ours to the best of our ability, even after they have fallen away. He never gave up on his children, so we must not give up on ours either.

So, if you have been sitting around worrying, regretting, or mourning over her mistakes or, worse yet, over your mistakes, please realize that there is a proper time for grief, but there is also a time to move forward with a new plan. If you have been stymied by self-doubt and second-guessing about decisions that you made in the past, it is time to stop those defeatist behaviors. Realize that the only reason to mentally revisit a mistake is so that you can avoid making it again in the future. Any time spent beyond that is a waste. Now, here are some practical ideas for interacting with a troubled daughter.

LOOK PAST THE REBELLION

Many of us are familiar with the biblical story of the prodigal or wayward son. It features a youngster who leaves home for a time of wild living. Eventually, the child realizes his mistake and wants to come home. Upon return, the young one finds his father waiting and watching. Rather than a stern lecture, the wayward child receives the father's blessing.

The good news about this story is that it reminds us that there comes a time when even the most rebellious young person comes to his or her senses and wants another try at a normal life. This should give hope to so many parents whose girls have chosen the wayward road. Please do not give up. Like the father in the story, keep watching down the road for her return.

Also, keep in mind that there are two key people involved in the reconciliation process: the father and the child. When the dad saw his son attempting to return home, he had every right to go down the road and angrily berate him with several years' worth of "I told you this would happen!" However, he did not.

Instead, the Bible tells us that the father saw his wayward child when he was *still far away* and ran to him, kissed him, and honored him with a robe and a special ring of authority. This is a model for all of us to follow. Can you picture how the child looked after a long time of wild living, poverty, and filth? Can you imagine how the boy smelled after literally living with pigs? Yet the father ran to him and kissed him.

Clearly, the father's unconditional love helped him see what others missed when they looked at this wayward child. As only a parent can, the father looked *past* the filth and saw all of the potential, the promise, the gifts, and the calling that a sovereign God had placed within the child. With sadness the father saw the weariness in his young man's eyes and the wounds on his body that inevitably come from a hard life on the road. However, despite the scars, he knew that there was once again hope for the future. This was well worth celebrating!

KEEP HOPE ALIVE!

Like the father in the biblical account, many dads today have daughters who have already left home, either physically or emotionally. Often, the parents of these wayward ones feel that they must wait passively and hopelessly for their child to reconnect. This is not the case. While these seem like the bleakest times, there are several reasons to remain hopeful.

First, if your daughter has rebelled and left home, it is helpful to realize that her Creator loves her more than you do. Your child is first and foremost a creation of God, and therefore, despite her waywardness, the young woman will always have her heavenly Father's attention.

Second, even if your daughter has gone to a distant land, you can still reach her with prayer. "Watch and pray" is a much better strategy than "fret and worry." Eventually, you will see her coming down the road. Do not stop watching and do not stop praying until she is home.

Third, each of us was created with a desire to know who we are, where we are from, and why we are here. No one ever found his true identity in wayward living, and no one ever puts down lasting roots in a pig pen. Eventually, like the younger sibling in the parable, your child will desire to reconnect with her family. When—not if—this happens, do not ask questions. Just run to her, hug her, and then begin to put together a plan for her future.

Remember, the father in the biblical account held the celebration for his child *before* there was any proof that he had truly changed. Therefore, if you wait to celebrate the return for your daughter until after she has her life totally together, you will never hold one. There is no reason to wait.

Without question, a transitional event itself is the key to much of your daughter's future. Perhaps for the first time in her life, she will be honored just for being a woman who carries within her God's irrevocable call. With her harsh life experiences as a backdrop, a wayward daughter is able to understand the two basic paths that everyone chooses between. One leads toward maturity, responsibility, and lasting satisfaction. The other leads toward further irresponsibility, temporary pleasures, and lasting regret. She will appreciate another chance to pursue the proper path.

DEALING WITH A WAYWARD DAUGHTER

The very first thing that the father or mother of a wayward daughter must do is to look inside to determine the condition of his or her own heart. This is a time to get rid of all guilt, anger, bitterness, and desire to get even with this daughter for any and all grief that she has caused. Once this is accomplished, things get very interesting.

If you are able to contact your daughter, do so. Attempt to reconcile the differences you may have and begin to rebuild your relationship. Forgive her *now* for whatever grief or embarrassment she has caused you. Our society has made it easy to divorce our spouses, but fortunately, it has not yet figured out a way for us to "divorce" our children. She is still your daughter! If out-of-sight becomes out-of-mind, your mind is on too many other things that are not nearly as important as your child.

Please do not think I am being insensitive to the nearly unbearable grief that our daughters can bring into our lives with wrong choices. Over the years, I have worked in prisons and with programs for troubled youth. Through those experiences, I have heard every imaginable horror story about family breakdown. I have spoken with many parents whose lives were shattered by the actions of their wayward daughters and sons. These were not children who simply ran away from home. Many cursed, mocked, robbed, shamed, or physically hurt their parents. Often, these young people ended up on the streets, in jails, or in other detention programs, seemingly out of reach. However, I am certain that our heavenly Father is able to touch a child in the darkest place on earth and break through to even the hardest heart. The bond that holds fathers and daughters together is never broken so severely that God cannot reconstruct it.

Here is the good news. Just as I have seen the many family tragedies, I have also seen a large number of miracles where seemingly hopeless young women were reconciled to God, their families, and their destinies.

As expected, there is a pattern to this process of restoration and reconciliation. Prayer is the foundation, and unconditional love is the motive. You must love your daughter despite what she has done. This never means that you must accept and love her sin; instead, it means that you do not allow her sin to cause you to stop loving *her.* Forgiveness is essential. Without it, you will simply remain a ticking time bomb, waiting to explode about your child's past transgressions at the worst possible time.

Finally, you will need to be patient if you are to avoid countless sleepless nights. Remember the father who watched for his son to come down the road and saw him when he was far off. My guess is the father looked in the daylight and slept at night. Keep the rest of your life moving forward as you patiently wait. Keep watching, praying, and loving. Pour out your love and attention on the family members who remain under your roof. If you have some extra time, get involved in a men's ministry to youth in your church or community. Your interaction with other families in need will release the compassion in you and bring great comfort to them. Then, when your child does come back, *immediately* make your plans to restart her on the journey to mature adulthood.

19

CELEBRATIONS FOR A WAYWARD DAUGHTER

WAYWARD DAUGHTERS AND SONS NEED HELP to get back on track. While there is not a systematic A-B-C approach to this, there are certainly some foundational principles that can be embraced. Again, one of the most powerful principles is that the parent must set the tone for the new relationship. That tone must be clear, and it must be based on unconditional love. Certainly, there are times when tough love must be employed for the protection of those involved. Love does not mean tolerating destructive or illegal behavior. However, love *does* mean that the focus is on bringing the young person back to her senses and back into God's plan for her life. No amount of shouting, threatening, or intimidation has ever helped someone regain their footing and sense of identity. Instead, that is accomplished by love, patience, and a series of gentle reminders of who the young person truly is.

As you walk this rocky path, please remember two things. First, it is never too late for God to turn the situation around. Second, it is not about you. You are the responsible, rational adult in this situation. Realize and accept the fact that you may need to sacrifice some sleep, work time, and money to see that your daughter comes "home." It is all about getting her young life turned around. At the appropriate time, a rite-of-passage ceremony can serve as a powerful transition point in the process.

Planning a rite of passage for a daughter who has lived in a wayward condition for any length of time will require a different mindset. Here are a few suggestions on how to proceed.

RECOGNIZE HOW MUCH YOUR DAUGHTER HAS ALREADY CHANGED

Understand that your daughter is not the same little girl she was before. Like Eve after the fall, her eyes have been opened to things that she was never created to see. Her mind may be filled with what was previously unthinkable. Drug abuse, sexual encounters, drunkenness, crime, rejection, and violence all cut deeply into a young woman's soul. They may cloud her view of even the most sincere efforts to help her regain her spiritual and relational footing, so remember to be patient.

This means that you may not get the reaction you are looking for when you begin the process of reconnecting with her. The concepts of lifelong mentoring, intentional blessing, and rites of passage may be foreign to your child, and it will naturally take time for her to adjust to them. Remember, mentoring, blessing, and hosting a celebration for the young woman is the right thing to do, regardless of her initial reaction. The wayward child may reject initial efforts to mentor her, since she has made many of her own decisions up to that point. Also, understand that words of blessing and affirmation may feel disingenuous to a young woman unraveling the chains of guilt and shame. That is all right. Keep blessing her. On the evening of her celebration, a prodigal may look disinterested in the letters and gifts that are brought to her and may lack the social graces to even thank the attendees. Again, keep your expectation realistic and your own emotions in check. As time passes, the plan for her maturity will work, and in the end your daughter will look fondly back on her celebration. The letters and gifts will become treasured keepsakes that God will use to encourage her when no one else is looking.

AVOID A BIG SURPRISE

I would not recommend that you surprise a wayward child with a celebration. My inclination is to let her know well beforehand that you have a gathering planned in her honor so she can adjust to the concept. She will probably think long and hard about it. A surprise may be too much for her to handle emotionally and could make her feel very uncomfortable.

INVITE JUST THE RIGHT WOMEN
TO PARTICIPATE IN THE CELEBRATION

When planning a celebration for a wayward or troubled daughter, I would also prayerfully consider whom to invite and, just as important, whom *not* to invite. You do not need a friend or relative using the celebration as an opportunity to "set your girl straight."

Quite frankly, the celebration isn't the time to push hard for your daughter's conversion to an active life of faith or to drag her back into the mainstream of society. Instead, it is a time to demonstrate your love for her and to show that a different way of life exists. It is a time to tell her positive truths about her own adulthood, show that an optimistic path still lies ahead, and lovingly encourage her that God and you are there for her. The celebration is a time to confirm and affirm that she is a woman. It is also a time for other women to talk about some of their own mistakes from the past and share how God helped get them back on track. This will help your daughter overcome guilt, shame, and sadness. It will also let her know that her situation is not unique, nor has she gone beyond the point of redemption.

RECALL THE GOOD TIMES

The celebration for a wayward daughter is also a time to rekindle good memories from the past. I realize that you may have to go back years to remember a time when your relationship consisted of more than shouting matches and slamming doors. However, nearly every family has some special moments from the past that can unlock even the hardest hearts. Perhaps it was a camping trip, particular holiday tradition, or a vacation that occurred more than a decade earlier. The list of possible positive memories is extensive. It may be reflections of quiet moments that father and daughter spent on a couch together watching television. A good report card or her first goal scored in competition may be milestones worth revisiting. Your daughter's talent as an artist, singer, and so on are positive things to be remembered. An old videotape or photo album of her childhood could be brought out and utilized as points of fond reflection. Any of these mile markers from the past will help her to realize that her life has not been all bad; she once knew happier times.

Regardless of what your daughter has experienced during her time of waywardness, know that God has made sure that some good memories are safely stored inside her mind and that they will reappear with just a gentle nudge. Your job is to lovingly wake her from the temporary "amnesia" that seems to afflict so many wayward girls. One of the most vital messages for your daughter to hear is that God is willing and able to create a new beginning for any woman who has the courage to ask him for it. In his written Word, God promised that nothing would separate his children from his love; and with God, all things are possible. You must give your daughter sufficient hope to overcome the feelings of loss, shame, guilt, and despair that often walk alongside a girl returning home from her time of waywardness.

KEEP AN OPEN MIND ABOUT THE RESPONSE

I want to encourage you to prepare for and host your daughter's celebration without prejudging how she, or you, will respond. Let's start with you. Be prepared for some emotions to be stirred and some tears to flow. On the day of her celebration, it is difficult to predict how your daughter will react. She may seem upbeat and happy, or she may appear sullen, depressed, or disinterested.

It may seem simplistic to say that every wayward child will respond either very positively or very negatively to a celebration. However, remember, these young women have been living a life of extremes. Some of them may become angry because the celebration is showing them what they have been missing. If they feel too "dirty" to accept the unconditional love offered, they may aggressively reject all the attention. Others may think it is too late for their lives to change. Some may act apathetic and show little emotion at all. Be mentally and emotionally prepared for any of these responses.

It is good to keep in mind that a celebration is simply the door to maturity, not the final destination. A girl may respond positively to the celebration but have no idea how to go about changing after the event is over. She may need many more months or years of your support, mentoring, and blessing before she can fully incorporate the message of the celebration into her life.

Regardless of the initial emotions displayed during her special event, your daughter's life will probably move in one of two essential directions. The first possibility is that she will immediately desire a better way to live, run to you, and ask for forgiveness, and you will move on with life together. The celebration will be the key to returning her to her family, society, and the path that God has for her life. If that happens, it will be wonderful, and I have no doubt that many families will see this occur. However, it is also possible that your child will take more time to pull away from the bad habits of her past. There may not be an instant rekindling of love between parent and daughter. Please remember that the cycle of sin, lack of trust, guilt, and shame often causes girls to guard their emotions to prevent anyone from seeing inside. If this happens, do not despair or accept the lie that your renewed commitment to mentoring, blessing, and the celebration has somehow failed. You have planted wonderful seeds that will grow within your daughter. In time, they will bring forth a harvest of maturity and restored relationships. Even if some aspects of your daughter's behavior seem to worsen after the celebration, you still have released the incredible power of a blessing into her life. The celebration will remain as an unmistakable sign of your devotion to your daughter that can never be taken away. God will cause the event to act like a wonderful flower that grows in your daughter's soul and blooms at just the right time.

PART 6

❧

NEW HOPE
FOR
WOUNDED
DADS

20

HEALING
A WOUNDED
HEART

OKAY, DAD. Now we have laid out a plan to reach, raise, love, and bless the daughters in your life. There is only one other thing to address before you are ready to implement the plan. That is your heart.

HEALING A WOUNDED HEART

Fact: every man, woman, and child has been wounded in this life. The severity of the wounds varies; some are shallow and temporary, others are deep and longer lasting. Often, a few of the wounds in life are physical: burns, breaks, and bruises. The sticks and stones variety. They typically leave a scar or limp, which elicits sympathy, concern, and compassion from others. However, another kind of injury leaves no outward sign of affliction—an emotional wound. This sort bypasses our skin and bones, lodging deep in our souls. Left untreated, these wounds send damaging signals to our minds, wills, and emotions. No one is immune or protected from such attacks.

"I have been wounded...so what?"

This is a great question for a father to ask. Especially those that are functioning quite well today. So what? The answer is simple. Your wounds *always* impact the way that you interact with others, especially your children. If you choose to remain wounded rather than healed, it is highly likely that you will cause some form of damage in your relationship with your own daughters. That is just the way it works. Conversely, if you choose to let God heal your wounds and deal with the issues of your past, it is just as likely that you will strengthen your relationships and bring healing to the children under your care.

Fortunately, God made human beings with an amazing capacity to overcome tremendous pain and still manage to function. Unfortunately, we often use this ability as an excuse to ignore our wounded condition. In fact, we can exist for years giving the same old response to others' questions of concern. "How are you?" they ask. We respond with the standard answer—"Fine"—even though we know that we are not. As men, we often believe that this approach to life is somehow honorable. You know, rugged individualists—"I gotta be me. I did it my way. It's just a scratch," and all of that. However, as we flounder around trying hard to convince others that we are "fine," we miss a very important fact. That is, we are not only responsible for our own lives; we are responsible for guiding the next generation into the future as well.

WHERE DID YOU GET THAT SCAR?

After years of involvement in college basketball, semiprofessional football, and dangerous jobs such as lumberjacking, I carry many physical scars on my body. Although most have faded with time, some are still visible. I acquired a dandy on my forehead many years ago after trying to make a quick exit from a car...through the windshield. Every now and then, someone notices the old wound and innocently asks, "Where did you get that scar?" For a moment, their question stuns me. Scar? What scar? It really does not register that I carry a scar that others can see. Why? Because the accident that caused the scar happened over thirty years ago. It no longer hurts. I went though the necessary process for healing. Ambulance ride. Hospital emergency room. Doctors. Nurses. Injections. Stitches (lots). Rest. Patience. Healing. If I force myself, I can dig far back into my memory and recall the car hitting the tree, the pain, the blood, the sirens, and all the rest. However, I am pleased to say that despite the scar, the injury no longer hurts me.

Healing is possible, no matter how deep the wound.

WHERE DID YOU GET YOUR SCAR?

The origins of our wounds and scars are many. Some came early in childhood. Harsh words and criticism from a parent. Rejection from classmates. Disappointments from a thousand possible origins. Recently, I read a sad and shocking letter in a newspaper column. A woman recollecting her eighth birthday party recalled a scarring event. Her parents had planned a wonderful gathering for her and all of her friends. The festive room was filled with everything that a girl could ever hope for on her special day. Balloons, presents, and the most beautiful cake that she had ever seen. It was covered with thick, white icing. Skillfully made, the cake had her name on it and was topped with an array of gorgeous flowers, created in pastel blue and green frosting. At just the right time, the girl's father called her over to the table and sat her in her chair. Just before her friends sang "Happy Birthday," her dad sweetly invited her to smell the flowers on her cake. In response, the young girl leaned forward only to have her father push her face into the sticky icing. Gasping for breath, she pulled back to hear her father and friends laughing uncontrollably at her misfortune. This young woman was deeply scarred by her father's cruel breech of trust. She described it this way, "My father thought he was being funny. Instead, he lost his daughter's love and trust that day." Oh, by the way, when she wrote those heartrending words, she was nearly eighty years of age. Untreated wounds do not heal by themselves.

High school is another prime place for picking up painful wounds and scars. Often this is the time when young people first fall in love, only to be rejected by the object of their affections. Peer pressure causes young people to do things that they later regret. Illegal drugs, alcohol abuse, and loss of virginity are all too common during this turbulent time. Other wounds happen later in life but slash just as deeply. Disappointments in college. The breakup of a marriage. Loss of a child. Death of a parent. Abuse from a superior at work. For some, the cruelest cuts from life are received at age forty, fifty, or beyond, when the reality of what was hoped for is eclipsed by what life has become.

At times, we can even believe that God himself has wounded us. I felt this very deeply when my beloved grandfather died many years ago. For nearly two decades, I was angry with God, thinking that he had somehow taken my hero away from me. I now realize that my heavenly Father did not cause my grandfather's death. Instead, his great love sustained me through that dark time and will continue to support me all the days of my life. However, despite the fact that God is love personified, many of us still mistakenly believe that he has somehow let us down. When this occurs, we often do the worst possible thing and run away from God instead of running *to* him. Bad idea.

OUR RESPONSE TO PAIN

Our responses to pain vary widely. Some of us actually seem to function well despite the ache inside. Others sink into deep discouragement and depression. Many drown their sorrows in a variety of substances that numb the mind and suppress the soul. Still others look for ways to disengage from the responsibilities of life, hiding behind hobbies, blaring televisions sets, or endless hours logged in cyberspace. Countless men and women try to dull their pain by working long hours, as if somehow a promotion or more money will heal their wounded hearts. Many, like vicious dogs abused by cruel owners, lash out at those closest to them, becoming abusive to spouses and children alike. Sadly, for some, the pain is so great that they abandon their families and homes. The result is predictable. A new cycle of wounds bleeds the vitality from the next generation.

WE WERE MADE IN WHOSE IMAGE?

Unfortunately—or perhaps by divine design—each of us must face the demons from the past that plague us before we can successfully serve the next generation. Is this overstated? Hardly. If I fail to deal with my own issues of pain, rejection, abuse, and abandonment, I then struggle to help the next generation with theirs. If I fall short in my quest to find my own God-given identity, I will likely leave my sons and daughters with a distorted sense of identity for themselves.

The Bible makes it clear that we all were made in *God's* own image. Therefore, we should strive to help our children become godlier in their actions, motives, and character. However, when our *own* self-image is faulty or damaged, we tend to push our sons and daughters, consciously or unconsciously, into *our* image of what they should look and act like.

WARNING SIGNS

There are some easy-to-spot signs of wounds in people if you know where to look. For example, wounded women and men often wrestle with decision making—too risky. Wounded people fight against showing too much affection—sign of weakness. When wounded, we struggle to say simple things like "I love you" to those closest to us—might be rejected. I am convinced that much of our anger, discouragement, rage, depression, anxiety, and fear are rooted in past wounds rather than in current challenges.

To be sure, the wounds received in life do much more than just impede our forward motion. They change our very self-image. Words of undue criticism, condemnation, failure, and shame all distort the way that we see ourselves. This is even true of born-again believers. Over the years, I have encountered countless people of faith who wrestled with self-image, self-worth, and self-esteem. Despite all that God says about their being new creations, these troubled souls still hear the haunting voices of fathers, mothers, and others declaring them to be worthless, wounded, and weak. Words from long ago have turned into slowly festering wounds that are evident to all but themselves.

HEALING — A WAY OF LIFE

Once I realized that my current attitudes, actions, and words were influenced, at least to some degree, by things that happened in my past, I became much more reflective. This was especially true when I acted in a way that was contrary to my core values. For example, if I was unkind to my wife, impatient with my children, anxious or fearful about an upcoming event, or unforgiving toward another person who had wronged me, I would take time to look back in my past to see if I could find some underlying cause. I want to underscore that the reason for reflecting upon the past is not so that you have someone to blame for your current misery. Nor is it so that you can justify living your life in the gutter or soothe your conscience if you are knowingly doing something wrong. Instead, there are two primary reasons for looking back to discover the cause of your wounds. First, you should look back to help understand your reactions to life's challenges today. Anger, jealousy, fear, pride, and other negative emotions had to originate somewhere. Once you know the source, it is easier to deal with them. Second, you should look back so that you can better understand those who hurt you, and then forgive them so that you can be healed. Once you are healed, you are then free to lead the next generation with a pure heart and a clear conscience.

THERE ARE NO PERFECT PARENTS

It is important to understand that often the people who hurt us had no clue that their words or deeds did us any harm. In reality, there are no perfect parents, nor are there perfect siblings, or in-laws, or teachers, or coaches, or pastors, or friends. They—no, we—are all capable of wounding those around us intentionally or unintentionally. As a grown man, this truth is easy to accept. However, it can be extremely difficult for children to comprehend that Dad or Mom is flawed in any way. Parents appear much like God to small children. After all, Dad and Mom provide children with shelter, clothing, food, comfort, and protection from day one. They cry and we hold them. They get hungry and we feed them. They make a mess and we clean it up, and so on. Imagine the shock when they first learn that a father or mother is less than perfect. It really rocks a young person's world. For many, whatever Dad or Mom said was absolutely true and irrefutable. In the eyes of a child, Mom and Dad know all. Therein lies the problem for those men whose parents' words were used to wound, embarrass, or reject them. In these all-too-common situations, it takes the work of God and the support of trusted friends to bind up the wounds that have occurred.

At some point, we must all accept the fact that we were raised by mere mortals who did their best but often fell short of the goal. Once this truth is internalized, forgiveness can be extended, healing can come, and we can live life at a much higher level.

Even those of us who study this subject drop the ball at times. Here is a sad example of one parent's words and the wounds they caused...in my own family.

When he was eleven, my youngest son, Daniel, had an aversion to certain bugs. We live in the country, where there is no shortage of bees, wasps, and hornets, so I assumed that it was a childhood sting that caused my son's fears. At one point, I asked him to explain why he was so troubled by these winged tormentors and was surprised at what he said. Daniel quietly told me about one hot summer day when we were all out at the back pond getting ready for a swim. As a joke, one of his older brothers had sneaked up behind Dan and placed a large bug on his back. The insect, trying to avoid falling, did what bugs do. It dug into Dan's skin and held on. My young son recounted how his siblings laughed at his anxious attempts to be rid of the bug and how frustrated—and scared—Dan had become.

As he told the story, I found myself getting angry at my older boys for playing that sort of trick on Daniel. I mentally prepared to give them a lecture once we got together again to straighten them out. To think that my sons were capable of that type of insensitivity really bothered me. Why had they not considered the consequences of their actions? Had they not realized the damage their behavior could have done to such a young boy's psyche?

I was preoccupied with building my case against the heartlessness of my older sons when I suddenly realized that Daniel was still telling his story. He had more to say about the situation that left a wound in his tender heart that day. After he told of his frantic attempts to dislodge the bug and the laughter from his brothers, Danny finished the story with words that I will never forget.

"And, Dad, when all that was going on," he said quietly, "you just stood there."

When my son said that, I was shocked, crushed, and deeply saddened. After all, I would gladly give my life for him, and yet I had stood idly by instead of coming to his rescue when he needed me the most. I immediately asked Daniel to forgive me and continue to pray that God will heal the wound I unknowingly caused my beloved son one hot summer day. There are no perfect parents. It is easy to wound those entrusted to our care without even knowing that we did so. My dad did it to me, and I did it to my own son. Okay. That's my confession. Now, it is your turn. Who or what has wounded you? Most important, are you ready to be healed? If so, you will be a much better father to your daughter. There is no better time to start than right now.

THE HEALING
PROCESS

FORTUNATELY, FOR THOSE OF US WILLING to acknowledge that we have been wounded, there is some very good news. Regardless of who or what has wounded us, God is able to bring healing and restoration into our lives. Let me personalize that for you. *God is willing and able to heal and restore you!*

THE HEALING PROCESS

The process for this healing is simple and can begin immediately. It can be summed up in this short phrase: *Look in, look back, look forward, and look up.* By this, I mean that in order to be healed we must first *look inside* to see where we have been wounded. Next, we must *look back* to identify where the wounds came from. Then, we *look forward* to a life free from bitterness and full of compassion, especially for the next generation. From this perspective, we are ready to seek the healing that God's love and the support of others will bring. Finally, we *look up* to God, release forgiveness to those who wronged us, and then ask for his healing. Here is some more detail on how the process works.

Look In

We must acknowledge that we all carry some pain from the past. The key is to take time to do an inventory of your life and then honestly identify areas where the painful words and deeds of other people have wounded you. It can help to correlate this emotional process to what happens to us when we are physically harmed. When our body is injured, our brain reacts instantly to alert us to the pain so we can prevent additional trauma. Unfortunately, I have had numerous opportunities in my life to test this. My athletic career was laced with various injuries, including torn muscles in my shoulder, broken ribs, and countless sprains. My left ankle was most susceptible to sprains over the years. Each time it was injured, the process of healing and restoration was the same. First, I had to realize and acknowledge that I was injured. The intense pain made that part simple. Next, the ankle required complete rest in order to begin the healing process. This generally meant lying on the couch with my foot elevated for several days. Once I was finally able to put some weight on the ankle, out would come the crutches, and I would use them instead of putting my weight on the ankle. Finally, the crutches were laid aside, and I began to "walk" again. Those first few steps were always uncertain and scary. The fear of pain has a way of staying with us. However, I realized that eventually I would need to walk, so that I could then run, so that I could then get back into the game. Therefore, when faced with the choice of staying on the couch or getting up, I had to push past the pain and do my best to walk again. The "walk" after the injuries was always slow and accompanied by a noticeable limp. There was just too much pain for me to walk without favoring the ankle. Eventually the ankle healed, and I was completely whole once more.

It is much the same with emotional pain in our lives. Whatever the cause, it always results in an emotional limp that stays with us until we are healed.

For example, people who have suffered abuse or abandonment often withdraw from life or become calloused in order to avoid additional pain. In effect, they live life on the couch to prevent any further trauma. In like manner, a person who has known a great deal of rejection no longer cares to venture out into the world where he or she may be hurt again. People who have been criticized all their lives learn that the best way to avoid more wounds is to simply limp along without trying anything new. Life lived this way soon loses the vibrant colors created by God and devolves into a sullen, rainy gray. We know that the game is still going on around us, but we are afraid to jump back in. The risk of more pain is just too great...unless we are healed.

Please understand that an emotional limp remains even if we have an appearance of success in a variety of areas. Big house. Good job. Highly visible ministry. Busy times two. Are these all signs of health and wellness in a person today? Perhaps. However, what others often fail to see are the wounds that we carry—and hide—just under the surface. The busyness, the fast pace, the endless commotion may actually be smoke screens. For too many of us, this flurry of activity is just another way to hide, and hide from, our own wounds. Remember, without healing, a wounded man or woman limps forever.

If you are not sure about the exact cause of your limp, or whether you even have one, the following questions may help. How do you see yourself? Are you afraid to make mistakes? Are you anxious, fearful, and discouraged? Do you work too much? Can you show affection to those around you? Can you tell your family that you love them? What issues are you overly sensitive about? Where are you trying to unduly protect yourself? Do you have any problem praying to God? By looking in, we can find our wounds and identify the cause of our emotional limp. Once this is completed, we then search for the origins of the problems by looking back into our past.

Look Back

In order to locate the source of emotional pain, it is especially helpful to recall the type of home environment in which you were raised. Did your parents or other adults focus on strengthening your sense of a healthy identity? Was your life filled with mentoring, words of blessing, healing touch, and a rite-of-passage celebration? If it was, you are in a tiny minority and are very fortunate indeed. For most people raised during the past few generations, life was a wild mix of good, bad, and ugly. So please know that you are not alone.

Here are more questions to help you look back. Who or what were you afraid of when you were growing up? What memories haunt you? What makes you angry? Are there people in your life, past or present, that you find hard to forgive? Are you still trying to prove anything to anybody? If in doubt about any of these questions, you can simply pray and ask God to show you what has wounded you. They will be keys to your healing as you move forward.

As we reflect upon our early years, one very healthy conclusion to reach is that those who raised us did their very best, and chances are that those who wounded us were wounded themselves. Alcoholic fathers, abusive mothers, twisted relatives, and mean-spirited peers all did and said what seemed right at the time, regardless of how idiotic their actions seem now. Jesus provided a great model for us when, on the cross, he looked at his tormentors and asked his heavenly Father to "forgive them, for they don't know what they are doing" (Luke 23:34).

Because we live in such a "blame someone else for my problems" society, I want to repeat one very important thing here. The point in looking back and identifying the source of our wounds is *not* so that we can excuse our own poor choices and negative behavior. Nor is it to place the responsibility for our current missteps, errors, and sins on someone other than ourselves. The excuse that "my dad abused me, so I now must abuse my own children" does not fly in the light of the gospel and God's amazing power to transform us from darkness to light. The whole point in looking in and looking back is to help us understand *why* we think and do certain things. Once this is discovered, we then move quickly ahead with the healing process.

Look Forward

At this point in the process, we have looked in and looked back; now it is time to find our motivation for change by looking forward. We learn from the Scriptures that Jesus endured the pain of the cross *because of the joy set before Him* (Heb. 12:2). Does that sound strange? It should not. Jesus' joy rested in the fact that his sacrifice made a way for all humanity to be reconciled to our heavenly Father. In other words, he endured the pain so that the generations that followed could be whole.

In much the same way, we must make a choice. We can play it safe, limp along, and hope our sons and daughters somehow turn out all right. Or we can endure the temporary pain of the healing process so that we can think and act as leaders for those who follow. In Malachi 4:6, God clearly calls us to turn our hearts toward the next generation, and countless men are answering the call. Let us be certain that our hearts are pure and as whole as possible when we turn them. When compared with the joy of the next generation succeeding, the price we pay for our own healing is next to nothing.

Look Up

Once we understand the nature of our wounds and their origins, we do two things. First, we look up to our heavenly Father for the healing that only he can bring. Prayer for the healing of our wounds results in wonderful freedom and release from past hurts. Sometimes the healing is instantaneous, and other times that prayer initiates a slow and steady process toward wholeness. Second, we look up into the faces of those around us. Faithful friends, family members, clergy, and counselors can help us process all that we have experienced. Powerful healing continues when men and women bring their dark fears and wounds into the light of trusted counsel. In the Scriptures, we are admonished to confess our faults to one another *so that we may be healed* (James 5:16). God knew that from the very beginning, human beings would have a multitude of faults, weaknesses, and wounds, all requiring healing. God also knew that we would be reluctant to share our problems with others. The obstacles of pride, fear, and isolation have been around a long time. Fortunately, God also knew that once we overcame our fears and shared our secret wounds with others, we could then be healed.

FORGIVENESS BREAKS YOUR CHAINS

There is one vitally important part of this process that needs to be explored. Everything up to this point has been comparatively easy. Now comes the part of healing that can be a bit tougher. It involves forgiveness. Not only is this a foundational concept of biblical Christianity, but also it is an absolute essential for men and women wanting to be whole. Here is why.

We often struggle with the concept of accepting forgiveness. Some of us believe that we have done such terrible things that God could never forgive us. For those in this camp, it may be comforting to know that God himself said that *all* have sinned and come short of his glory. Your particular brand of sin is nothing new; it was just new to you. If you believe the lie that you have gone too far for a loving God to reach and forgive, you will never feel qualified to reach the next generation. Receiving God's forgiveness for yourself will begin the process of enabling you to forgive others. Without it, you will never start.

There is another important application of forgiveness. Some people willingly accept God's forgiveness for themselves; however, they are reluctant to offer that same forgiveness to others. This leads to a very self-centered, delusional way of thinking in which our blackest deeds are miraculously forgiven by God, but even the slightest sin against us is cause for eternal damnation of the offender. Sorry, that approach to life is not in the Book. God promised to *forgive us* our trespasses *as we forgive* those who trespass against us. Failure to forgive does incredible damage to the one holding on to the anger that often accompanies this troubling condition. We must understand that unforgiveness binds us to those that hurt us. It forges unseen chains that link our souls, thoughts—conscious and subconscious—and actions. Moreover, as long as those chains remain intact, we drag a host of bad memories and bitterness around wherever we go. That needs to stop…today.

FORGIVENESS — A PERSONAL EXAMPLE

I remember some years ago when I was deeply wounded by a supposed friend whom I helped out of deep financial troubles. My kindness and many thousands of dollars saved him and his family from ruin. However, once his crisis was averted, he repaid me by keeping all of my money and breaking off the "friendship." I confess that I burned with anger and bitterness over that situation for quite a few months. I knew the biblical mandate to forgive, but in all honesty, I simply did not want to do it!

After all, this man knowingly cheated me, and he deserved to be punished. For quite a long time, I held my feelings in. At least I thought I did. In reality, I was slowly pouring out my anger on those around me. I snapped at my wife and snarled at my children when they did little or nothing wrong. During that painful period, I rarely smiled and spent much time preoccupied with thoughts of revenge, retribution, and reprisal. Eventually, I swallowed my pride and shared my pain with some trusted friends who did what needed to be done. They got me to see that my original motives in helping the man were good—even if my judgment was lousy—and that God would somehow make the situation right. They finally helped me to express a prayer of forgiveness for the man and to put him into the hands of a fair and just God to receive his "reward" for his actions.

After praying, I initially felt nothing change. The tormenting thoughts still tried to invade my mind for several days. However, before long, I noticed that I went days without thinking about the situation. I even began to pray for the man and his family. Now that was a switch! Eventually, I came to a place where I could grow from the situation. Clearly, I had been too trusting and had failed to listen to others who had counseled me against helping this particular man who had cheated others in the past. Over time I have moved on and can honestly say that, while I still regret the whole situation, I am no longer bound to it by bitterness. God will deal with him. I have forgiven. I have moved on. You can, too.

Whether your wounds are large or small, new or old, you still need to come to the place where you forgive those who inflicted them, so that *you* can be free. Remember, your forgiveness does *not* mean that what happened to you was or is all right. It does not, in any way, justify the other person's actions. Nor does it remove the other person's guilt or responsibility to make restitution or offer an apology. Instead, your forgiveness does two simple things that will change the course of your life. First, it puts you back into right standing with God. Remember, in the Lord's Prayer we are told to ask God to forgive us our sins as we forgive those that sin against us (Luke 11:4). Forgive so that God forgives you. The second thing that forgiveness does is to set us free from entangling chains of bitterness, anger, and a whole host of other negative emotions. Once our hearts are clear, we can be filled with the true substance of God's kingdom, which is righteousness, peace, and joy.

I suppose that I could have gone on with life without extending forgiveness toward this man or the host of other folks who took more than they gave during our time together on this earth. However, had I failed to forgive, there is one thing that I am sure of. I would never have had the ability to love, mentor, and bless my own children or to properly love my wife. My own "issues" would have continued to cloud my thinking, distort my personality, and generate untold amounts of anger waiting to invade my home without warning. For all of us, it is time to forgive and move on.

BEFORE IT'S TOO LATE

Please do not think that this message about wounds, forgiveness, and healing applies to everyone other than you. In the years since we held the first rite-of-passage celebration for my oldest son, I have witnessed the spiritual and relational meltdown of no fewer than six of the men who participated in his event. At the time, these were men with vibrant faith and strong family ties. Just a few years later, several ended up having affairs, divorced, or in otherwise unimaginable situations. One of these men, a formerly trusted counselor and pastor, left his wife and ran off with a seventeen-year-old young woman that he had been "counseling." How could this happen to a person who loves God and has committed his life to the ministry, not to mention to his wife? Easy. He simply failed to deal with issues, hurts, wounds, and the pain that led him into such childish, thoughtless behaviors. Wounded people wound others. However, we have a choice in the matter.

So look up. God is able to hear about, understand, and deal with any and every situation that you have been through. Then, share your hurts, frustrations, and anger with the trusted people closest to you. They will not be shocked by your story. It will simply confirm that someone else has been through tough times and survived. In fact, they will be blessed by your openness, and you will be blessed by their acceptance and support.

Epilogue

THE KING
IS CALLING

I HOPE YOU ARE CONVINCED that the King is calling you to get involved with the next generation—starting with your own daughters and sons and then extending out to other young people who need your love, protection, mentoring, and guidance. Just like our warrior in the first chapter, we have no time to sleep or even to sit down for a rest.

THE POWER OF DAD

Can the presence of a father or father figure really have that great an impact? If you are still not sure, here are some final statistics from the National Fatherhood Initiative to help you decide:

- In the USA alone, 24 million children live absent from their biological father.
- An amazing 82 percent of girls who become pregnant as teenagers come from families where no father is present.
- Children who live absent from their biological fathers are, on average, at least two to three times more likely to be poor; to use

drugs; to experience educational, health, emotional and behavioral problems; to be victims of child abuse; and to engage in criminal behavior than those who live with their married, biological (or adoptive) parents.

This data should be sufficient for us to realize the devastating impact of fatherlessness. However, here is the bright side...

Children with involved, loving fathers are significantly more likely to do well in school, have healthy self-esteem, exhibit empathy and pro-social behavior, and avoid high-risk behaviors such as drug use, truancy, and criminal activity compared to children who have uninvolved fathers.

This is where you come in. A dad. A father. A warrior willing to step into the battle and swing his sword until the enemies of our children no longer raise their ugly heads. You are the answer, and now that the solution to our children's problems has been so clearly identified, this bleak picture can be changed. The destruction of our precious daughters and sons can end. All it takes is you. One on one. Generation after generation. Our children don't need famous figures they can worship. They need father figures they can love.

WE CAN TURN THE TIDE

Remember what happened when just one man, Jonah, walked through the city of Nineveh with a message of change? The whole city repented of its wicked ways. Imagine what will happen when thousands of godly men walk through our society with a message of positive change. When rites of passage, intentional blessing, and mentoring of the younger generation become a way of life for your home, your church, your neighborhood— then strength will return to our cities and our nations.

There is a move of God upon the earth today to restore what has been lost or stolen. Family. Faith. Fatherhood. Mentoring. It is God's desire that the hearts of the fathers be turned to their children and the hearts of the children turn to their fathers (see Malachi 4:6). This is achievable in our time. When fathers catch the vision, we can turn entire nations around within one generation. Only one thing can stop us: failing to start.

This week—no, today—I solemnly challenge you to turn off the television, put away your business planner, and prayerfully accept your truest vocation—that of a father. Take godly pride in the incredibly high calling to lead your family, to teach and to bless your daughters and sons.

Our opportunity to change the direction of an entire generation is very real. It just takes a few warriors to wake up and hear the call of the King. It takes *you* to do it. Nothing is more important. It is a high calling. It is the King's calling. It is a father's duty.

ABOUT THE AUTHORS AND THE MALACHI GLOBAL FOUNDATION

🌿 BRIAN AND KATHLEEN MOLITOR are the founders of the Malachi Global Foundation. This nonprofit organization is dedicated to the fulfillment of Malachi 4:6 and seeks to turn the hearts of the fathers to the children around the world. The Malachi Global Foundation works closely with churches and men's ministries to host conferences, seminars, and retreats for men, couples, and fathers/sons/daughters. It also produces a wide range of teaching materials in audio, video, and workbook formats to help parents implement strategies of lifelong mentoring, intentional blessing, and rites of passage for the children in their lives. Brian's book *Boy's Passage—Man's Journey* helped launch this ministry into many nations.

Brian is also the chief executive officer of Molitor International. His company specializes in consulting and training in interpersonal relationships, organizational development, team building, problem solving, and leadership coaching. He has produced and hosted numerous television programs on various topics including family building. He writes business columns for several magazines and produces many training manuals, videos, and audiotapes used by businesses, ministries, governments, and families throughout the world. Brian is also the author of *The Power of Agreement Unleashed* and numerous other books.

Before his present career, Brian worked as the director of a residential camp for troubled youth and as the director of a statewide men's prison

173

ministry. He and Kathy are the parents of four children: Christopher, Steven, Jenifer, and Daniel. As a dad, Brian enjoys coaching a number of sports, including his sons' basketball and junior-league football teams.

Kathy is a former registered nurse and administrator of a citywide health clinic. She has spoken at many churches and women's ministry group functions on the topics of marriage and child rearing.

For more information on the Malachi Global Foundation or to schedule a conference, seminar, or retreat for your church or men's group, please contact them by any of the following methods:

Malachi Global Foundation
1550 Collins Lane
Midland, MI 48640

Web site: www.malachiglobal.org
E-mail: info@malachiglobal.org
Toll-free telephone: 1-877-MALACHI (1-877-625-2244)
Fax: (989) 698–0469